D1128984

♡PEN EARTH

OPEN

WRITTEN BY **SARAH MIRK**
ILLUSTRATED BY **EVA CABRERA**
COLORED BY **CLAUDIA AGUIRRE**

LETTERED BY CRANK!
FLATTING ASSISTANCE BY ROCÍO SANCHEZ PEÑÚÑURI

EARTH

A LIMERENCE PRESS
PUBLICATION

Designed by **Kate Z. Stone** · Edited by **Ari Yarwood**

PUBLISHED BY LIMERENCE PRESS
Limerence Press is an imprint of Oni Press, Inc.

JOE NOZEMACK founder & chief financial officer
JAMES LUCAS JONES publisher
CHARLIE CHU v.p. of creative & business development
BRAD ROOKS director of operations
MELISSA MESZAROS director of publicity
MARGOT WOOD director of sales
SANDY TANAKA marketing design manager
TROY LOOK director of design & production
HILARY THOMPSON senior graphic designer
KATE Z. STONE graphic designer
SONJA SYNAK junior graphic designer
ANGIE KNOWLES digital prepress lead
ARI YARWOOD executive editor
SARAH GAYDOS editorial director of licensed publishing
ROBIN HERRERA senior editor
DESIREE WILSON associate editor
ALISSA SALLAH administrative assistant
JUNG LEE logistics associate
SCOTT SHARKEY warehouse assistant

1319 SE Martin Luther King, Jr. Blvd.
Suite 240
Portland, OR 97214

Limerencepress.com
Limerencepress.tumblr.com
@limerencepress

mirkwork.com / @sarahmirk
behance.net/evacabrera / @evacabrera
cargocollective.com/claudiaguirre / @claudiaguirre
@ccrank

First Edition: September 2018
ISBN: 978-1-62010-501-6
eISBN: 978-1-62010-502-3

1 3 5 7 9 10 8 6 4 2

Library of Congress Control Number: 2018939050

Printed in Hong Kong.

Open Earth, September 2018. Published by Limerence Press, Inc. 1319 SE Martin Luther King Jr. Blvd., Suite 240, Portland, OR 97214. Open Earth is ™ & © 2018 Sarah Mirk, Eva Cabrera, and Claudia Aguirre. Limerence Press logo and icon are ™ & © 2018 Oni Press, Inc. All rights reserved. Limerence Press logo and icon artwork created by Catherine Renee Dimalla. The events, institutions, and characters presented in this book are fictional. Any resemblance to actual persons, living or dead, is purely coincidental. No portion of this publication may be reproduced, by any means, without the express written permission of the copyright holders.

HONESTY
KEEPS US
ALIVE

Space--the vast, lonely, soundless void.
FORNIA
CALIFORNIA
Except when you live with your goddamn parents.

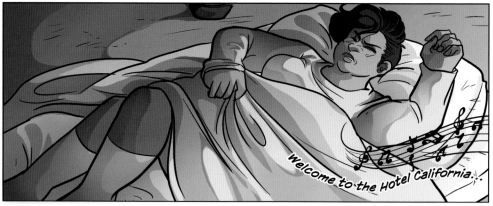

Welcome to the Hotel California...

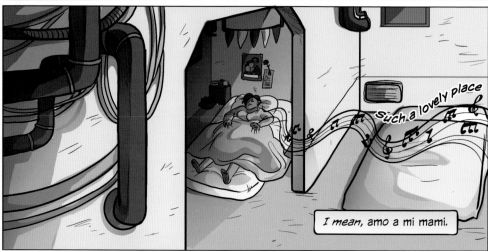

Such a lovely place

I mean, amo a mi mami.

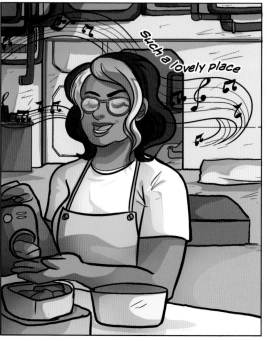

Such a lovely place

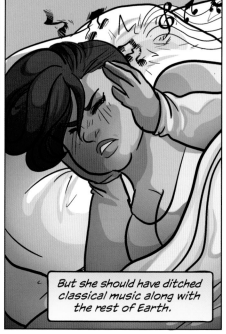

But she should have ditched classical music along with the rest of Earth.

Rigo!
Breakfast!

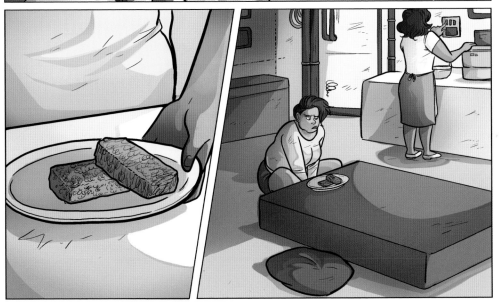

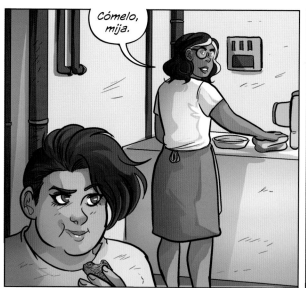

Cómelo, mija.

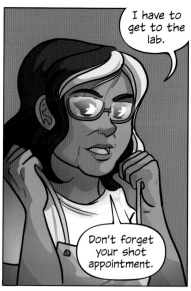

I have to get to the lab.

Don't forget your shot appointment.

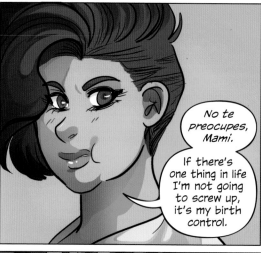

No te preocupes, Mami.

If there's one thing in life I'm not going to screw up, it's my birth control.

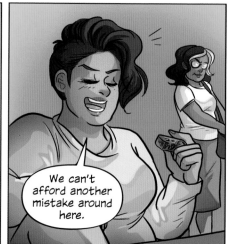

We can't afford another mistake around here.

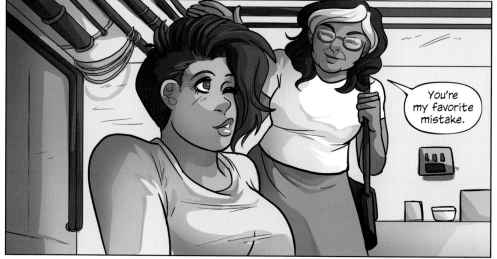

You're my favorite mistake.

I'm your only mistake.
Right?
Right?!
¡Claro!

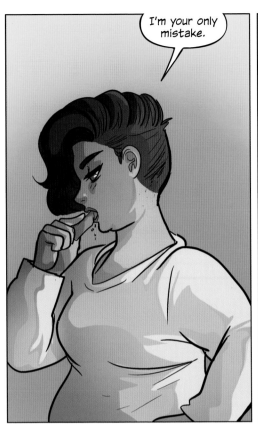

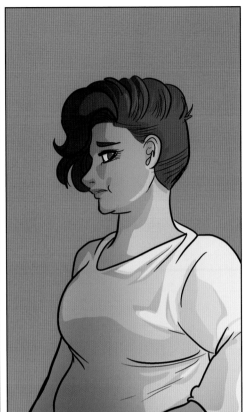

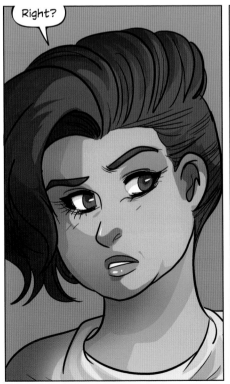

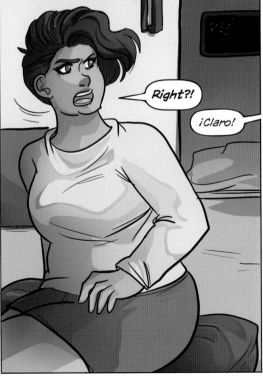

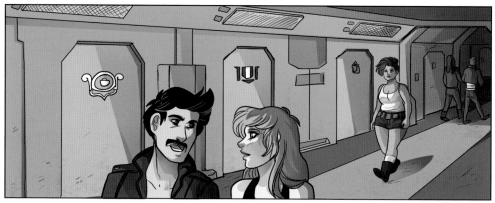

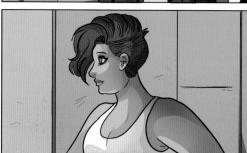

Serve the Greater Good

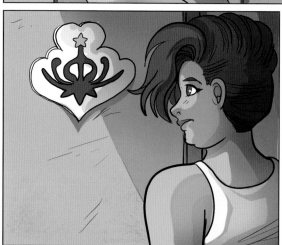

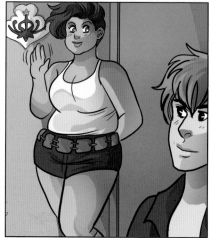

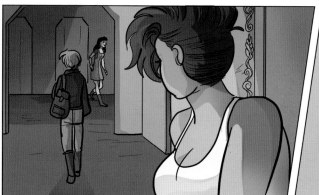

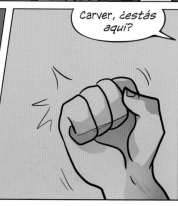

Carver, ¿estás aquí?

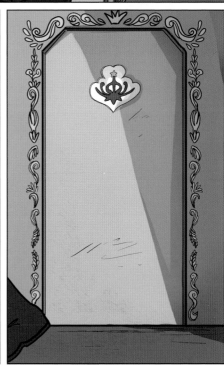

Buenas, Dad.
I'll grab your shot in one second, *cariño.*
Whose blood is that?
Mine.
Just checking nutrient levels.
Good news: still no scurvy in my future.
Dad, we're ***fiiiine.***
The farm has us totally nutrient balanced.

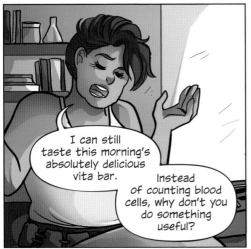

I can still taste this morning's absolutely delicious vita bar.

Instead of counting blood cells, why don't you do something useful?

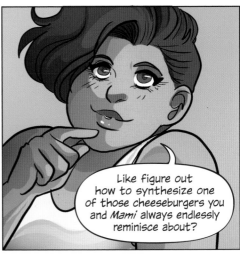

Like figure out how to synthesize one of those cheeseburgers you and *Mami* always endlessly reminisce about?

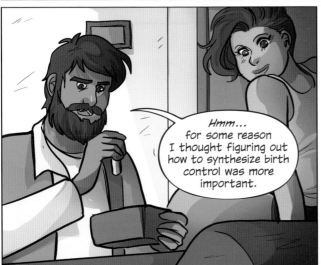

Hmm... for some reason I thought figuring out how to synthesize birth control was more important.

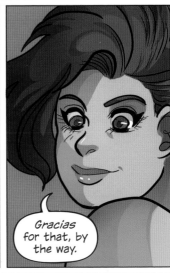

Gracias for that, by the way.

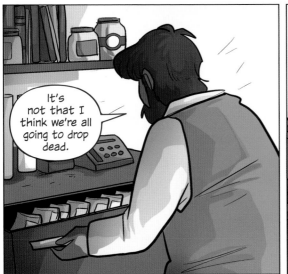

It's not that I think we're all going to drop dead.

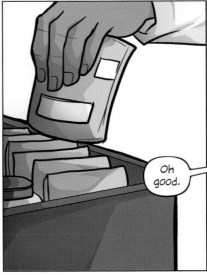

Oh good.

17

We just need to know if our bodies are changing.
We've only had 20 years so far.
Who knows what humans will be like by year 1000?
STERILIZE
I predict...
Hungry.

They'll probably have to readapt to Earth.
If they decide to go back.
They'll go back.
Ugh, this again.
The way you and *Mami* talk about Earth, I think we're better off up here.
It's a new start. It's exciting!
It's not a new start! We have to preserve our culture, we have to preserve our humanity.
It seems like it's those cultures that fucked the Earth up in the first place.

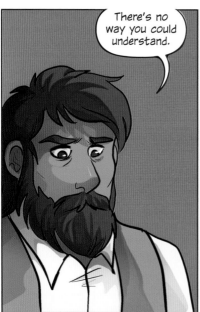

There's no way you could understand.

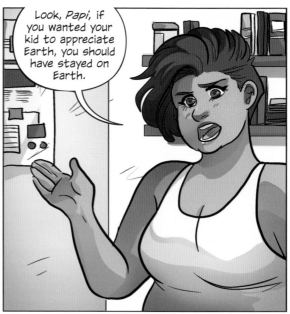

Look, *Papi*, if you wanted your kid to appreciate Earth, you should have stayed on Earth.

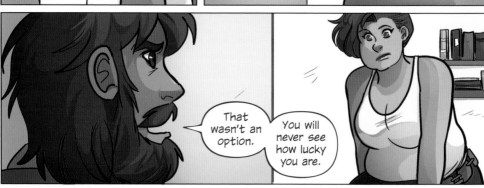

That wasn't an option.

You will never see how lucky you are.

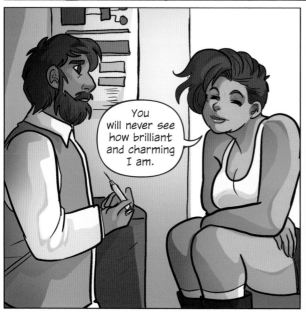

You will never see how brilliant and charming I am.

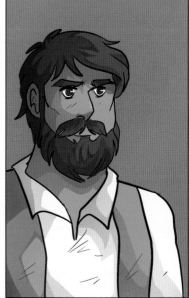

All I'm saying is, you don't have to be so serious about Earth-ways.
A little change is good, *viejo.*
I've had enough change!
Change means California Sur is underwater.
Change means everyone I knew is gone.

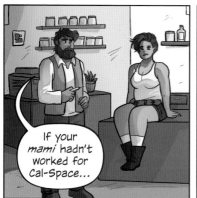

If your *mami* hadn't worked for Cal-Space...

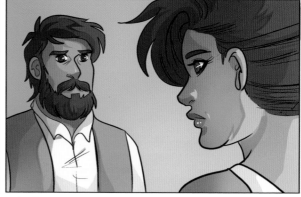

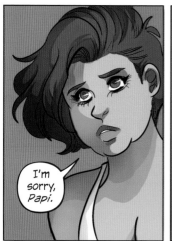

I'm sorry, *Papi*.

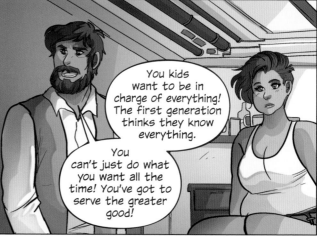

You kids want to be in charge of everything! The first generation thinks they know everything.

You can't just do what you want all the time! You've got to serve the greater good!

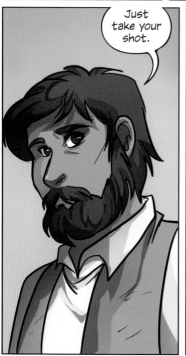

Just take your shot.

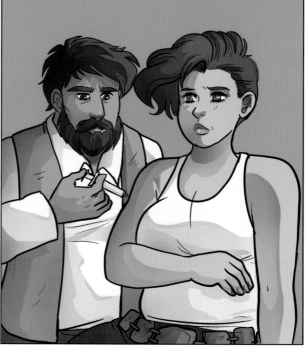

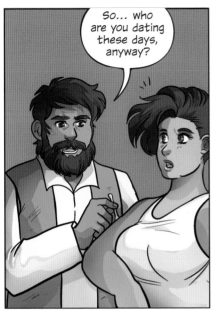

So... who are you dating these days, anyway?

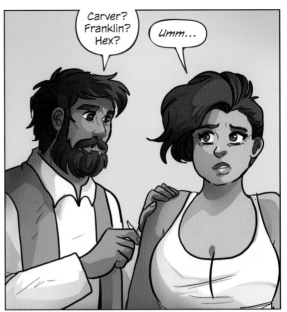

Carver? Franklin? Hex?

Umm...

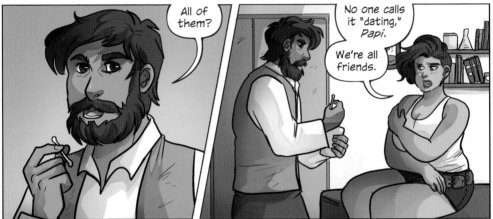

All of them?

No one calls it "dating," Papi.

We're all friends.

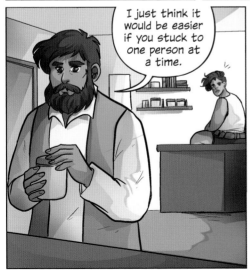

I just think it would be easier if you stuck to one person at a time.

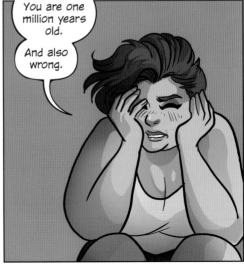

You are one million years old.

And also wrong.

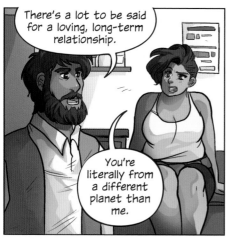

There's a lot to be said for a loving, long-term relationship.

You're literally from a different planet than me.

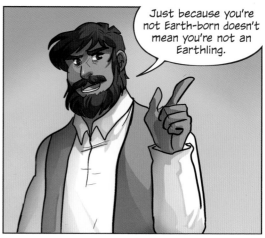

Just because you're not Earth-born doesn't mean you're not an Earthling.

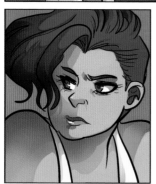

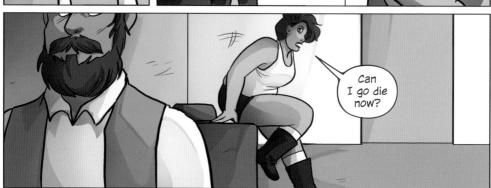

Nevermind, I'll just find out from someone else.

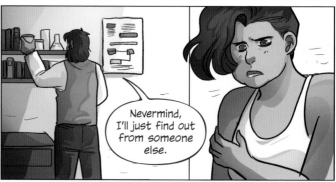

Can I go die now?

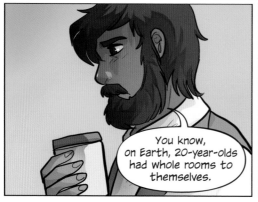

You know, on Earth, 20-year-olds had whole rooms to themselves.

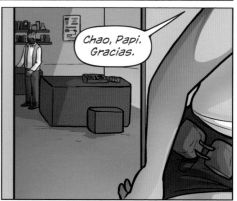

Chao, Papi. Gracias.

CALIFORNIA

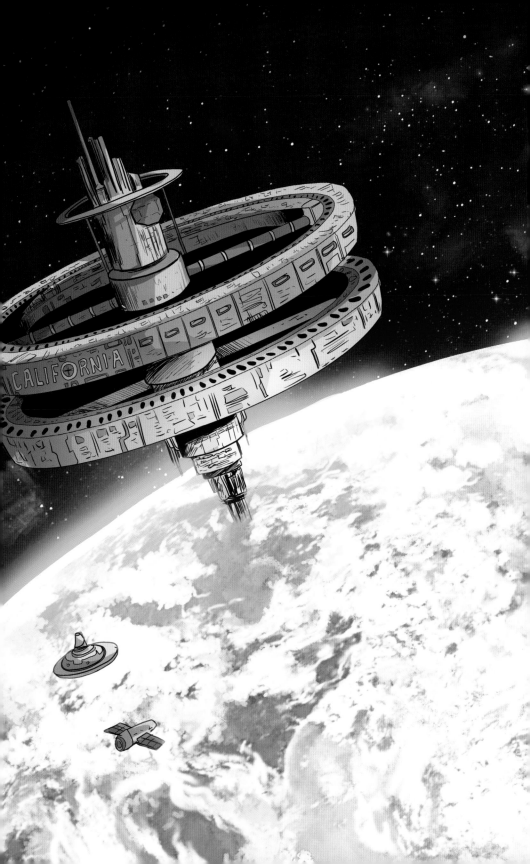

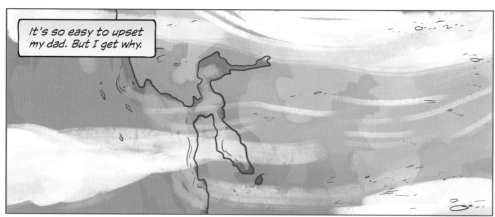

It's so easy to upset my dad. But I get why.

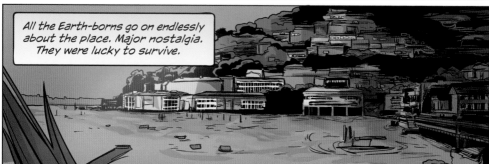

All the Earth-borns go on endlessly about the place. Major nostalgia. They were lucky to survive.

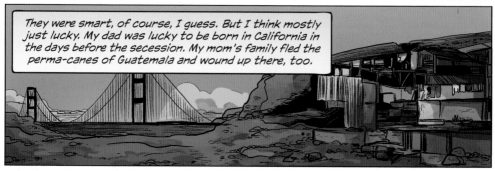

They were smart, of course, I guess. But I think mostly just lucky. My dad was lucky to be born in California in the days before the secession. My mom's family fled the perma-canes of Guatemala and wound up there, too.

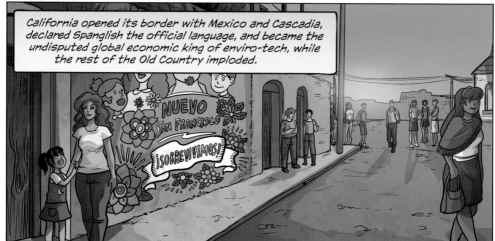

California opened its border with Mexico and Cascadia, declared Spanglish the official language, and became the undisputed global economic king of enviro-tech, while the rest of the Old Country imploded.

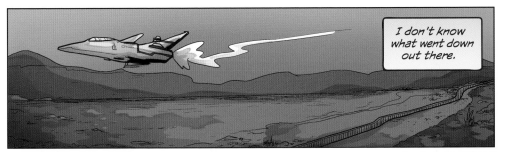

I don't know what went down out there.

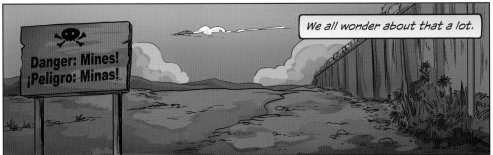

Danger: Mines!
¡Peligro: Minas!

We all wonder about that a lot.

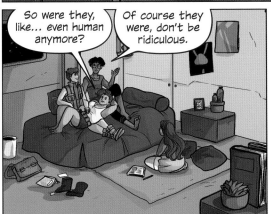

So were they, like... even human anymore?

Of course they were, don't be ridiculous.

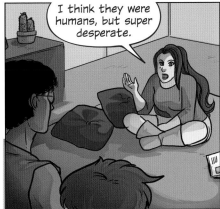

I think they were humans, but super desperate.

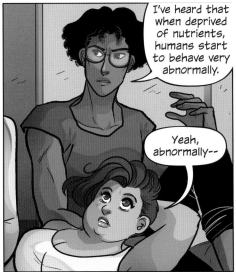

I've heard that when deprived of nutrients, humans start to behave very abnormally.

Yeah, abnormally--

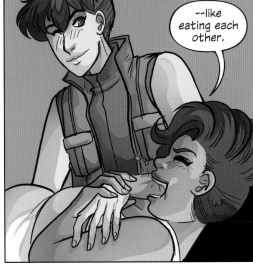

--like eating each other.

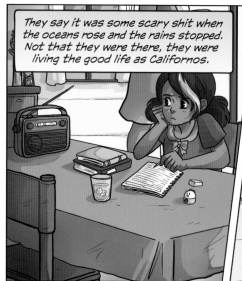

They say it was some scary shit when the oceans rose and the rains stopped. Not that they were there, they were living the good life as Californos.

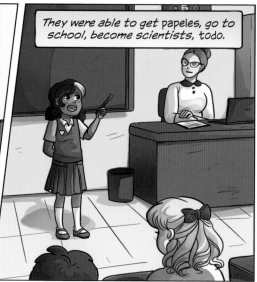

They were able to get papeles, go to school, become scientists, todo.

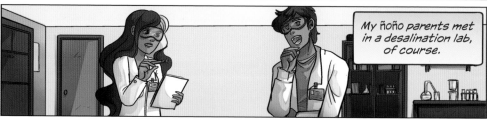

My ñoño parents met in a desalination lab, of course.

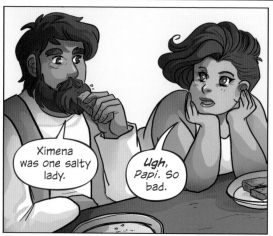

Ximena was one salty lady.

Ugh, Papi. So bad.

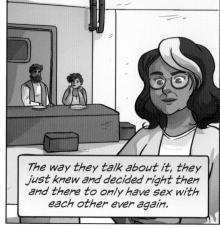

The way they talk about it, they just knew and decided right then and there to only have sex with each other ever again.

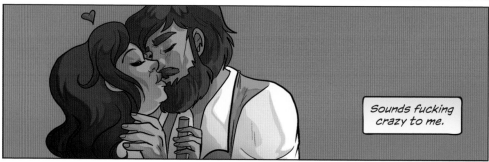

Sounds fucking crazy to me.

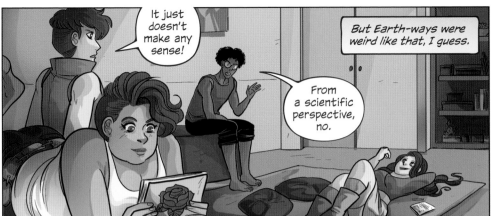

It just doesn't make any sense!

But Earth-ways were weird like that, I guess.

From a scientific perspective, no.

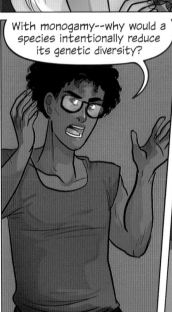

With monogamy--why would a species intentionally reduce its genetic diversity?

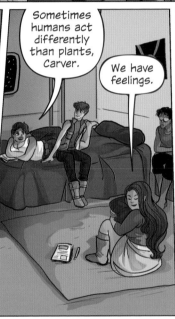

Sometimes humans act differently than plants, Carver.

We have feelings.

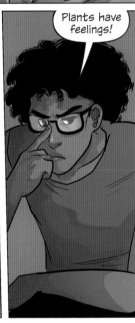

Plants have feelings!

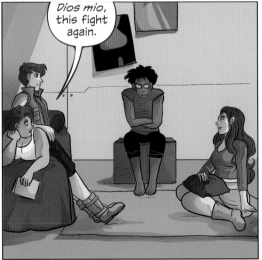

Dios mio, this fight again.

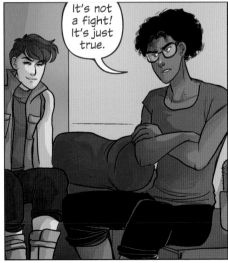

It's not a fight! It's just true.

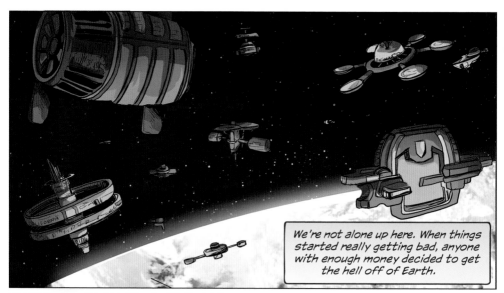

We're not alone up here. When things started really getting bad, anyone with enough money decided to get the hell off of Earth.

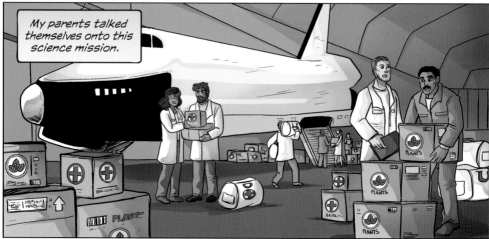

My parents talked themselves onto this science mission.

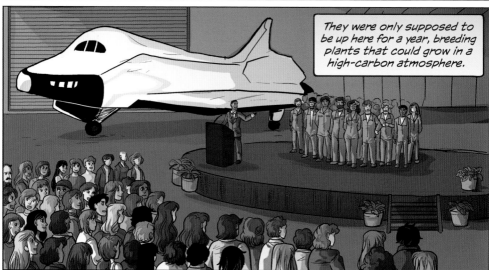

They were only supposed to be up here for a year, breeding plants that could grow in a high-carbon atmosphere.

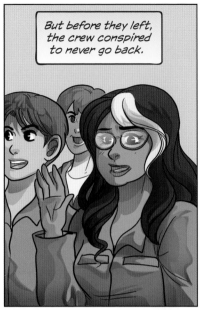

But before they left, the crew conspired to never go back.

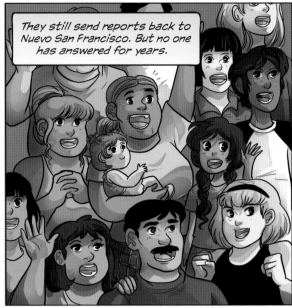

They still send reports back to Nuevo San Francisco. But no one has answered for years.

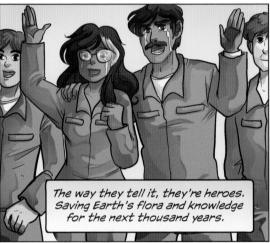

The way they tell it, they're heroes. Saving Earth's flora and knowledge for the next thousand years.

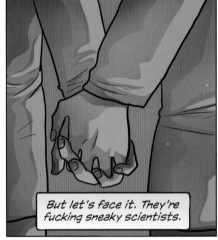

But let's face it. They're fucking sneaky scientists.

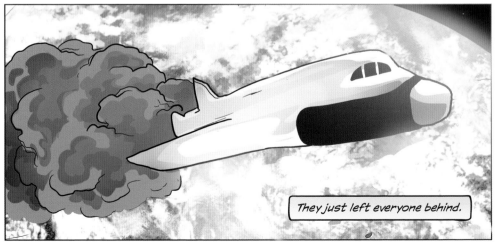

They just left everyone behind.

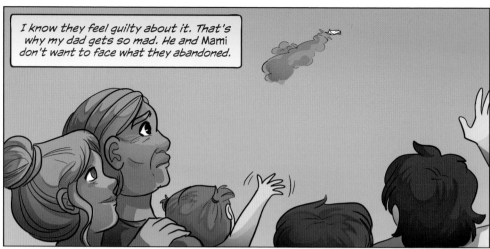

I know they feel guilty about it. That's why my dad gets so mad. He and Mami don't want to face what they abandoned.

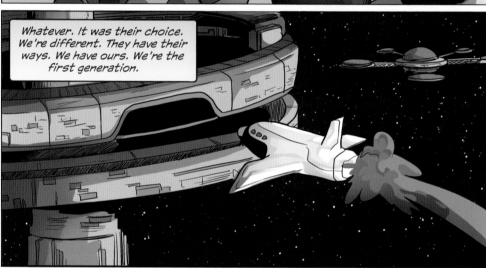

Whatever. It was their choice. We're different. They have their ways. We have ours. We're the first generation.

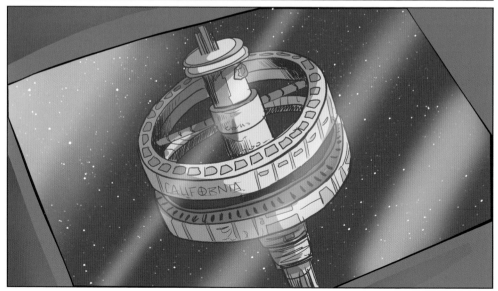

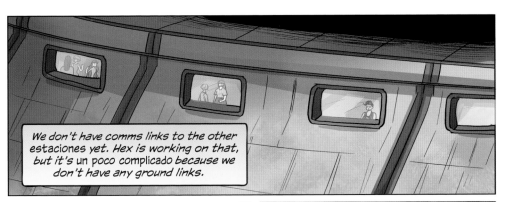

We don't have comms links to the other estaciones yet. Hex is working on that, but it's un poco complicado because we don't have any ground links.

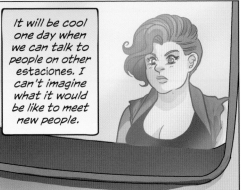

It will be cool one day when we can talk to people on other estaciones. I can't imagine what it would be like to meet new people.

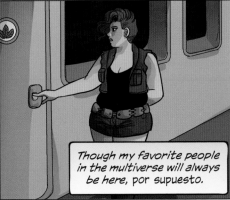

Though my favorite people in the multiverse will always be here, por supuesto.

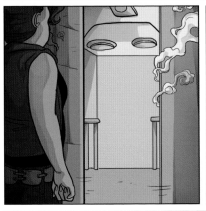

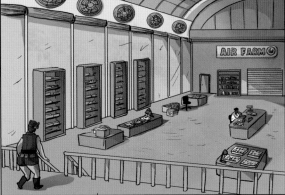

AIR FARM

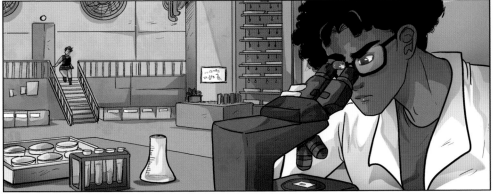

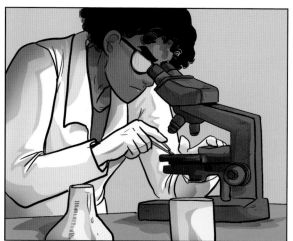

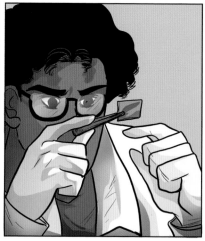

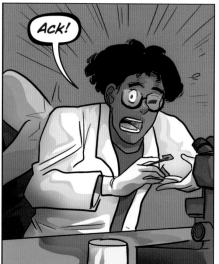

Ack!

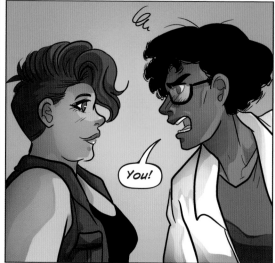

You!

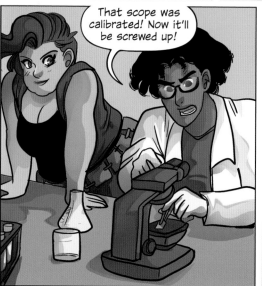

That scope was calibrated! Now it'll be screwed up!

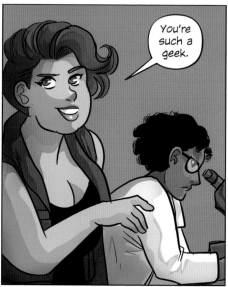

You're such a geek.

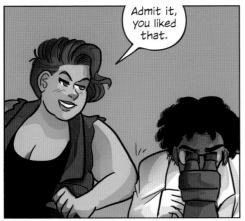

Admit it, you liked that.

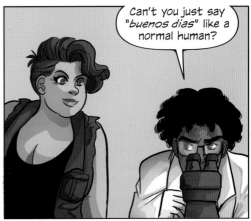

Can't you just say "buenos dias" like a normal human?

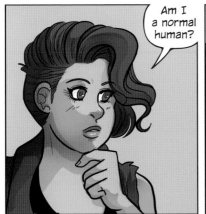

Am I a normal human?

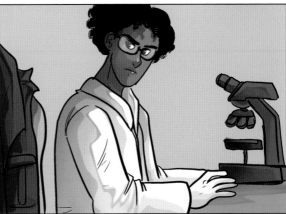

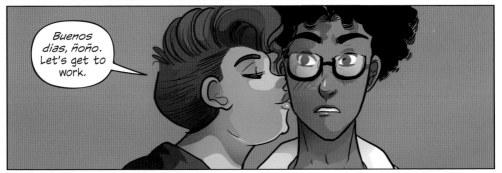

Buenos dias, ñoño. Let's get to work.

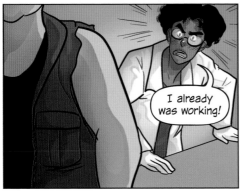

I already was working!

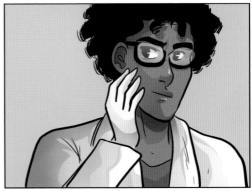

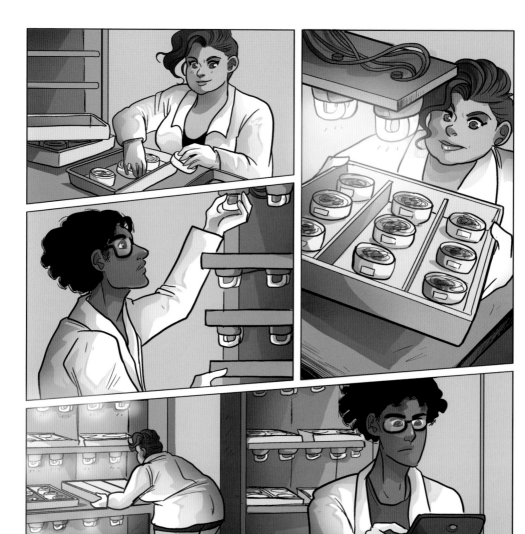

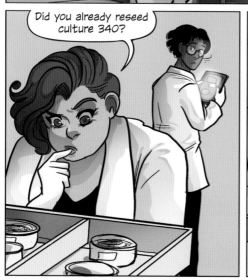

Did you already reseed culture 340?

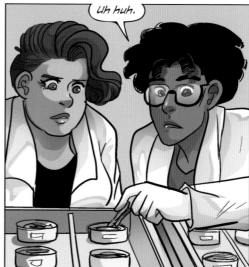

Uh huh.

So we're pretty much done for the morning, then.
Uh huh.
So, want to go check the supply room?
SUPPLY ROOM
SUPPLY ROOM
THUMP
Chingado!
It's okay.

You like this?
Yeah, I do.
Too much?
No, perfect.

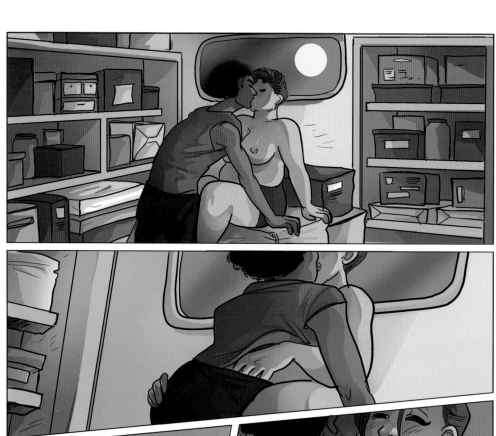

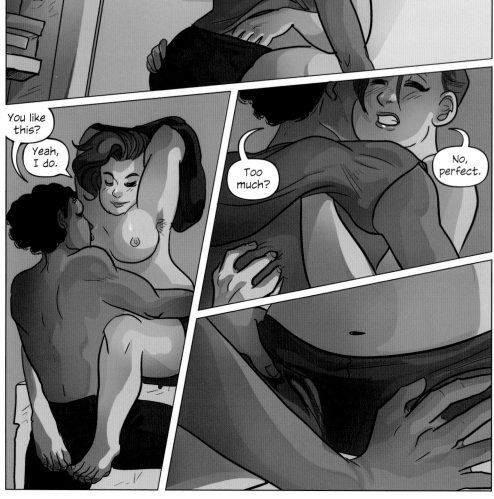

You have the best ass.
Really, the best?
Voted number one among the sole survivors of humanity.
Ha! Come here.

Gah!

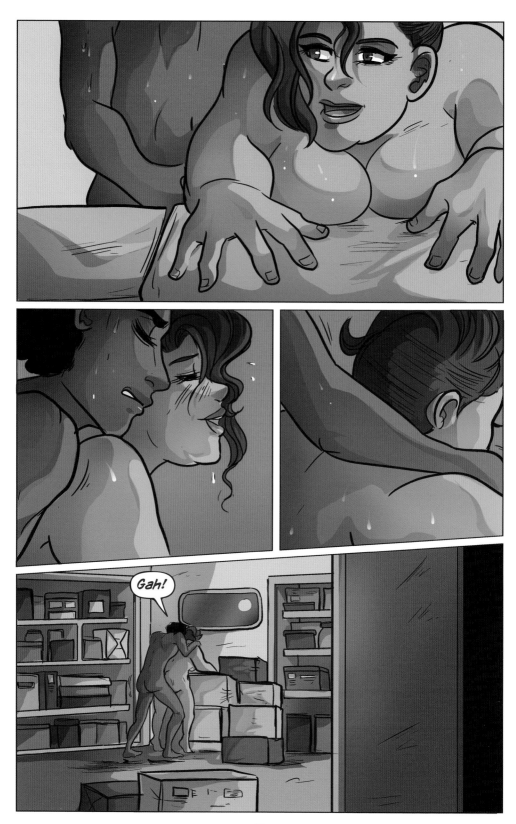

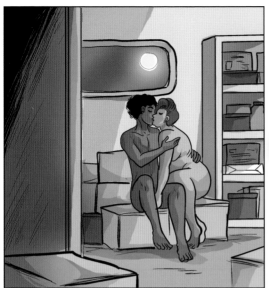

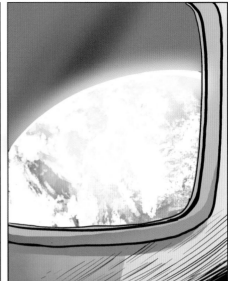

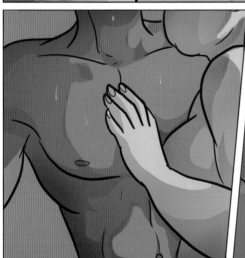

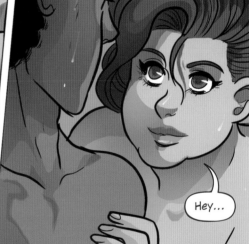

Hey...

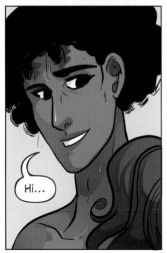

Hi...

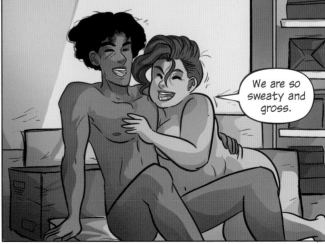

We are so sweaty and gross.

Te quiero.
I love you, too.
Is that stupid?
No.
You're just so warm.
One of my few talents.

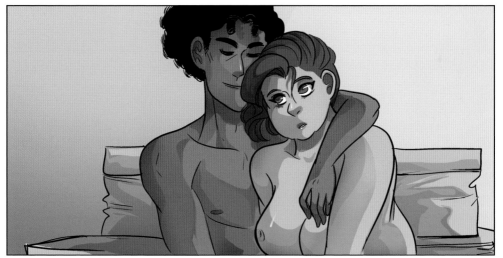

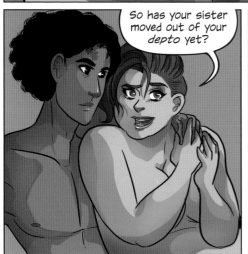

So has your sister moved out of your *depto* yet?

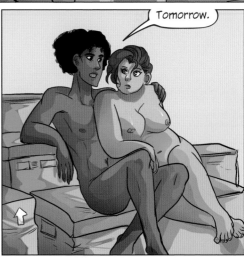

Tomorrow.

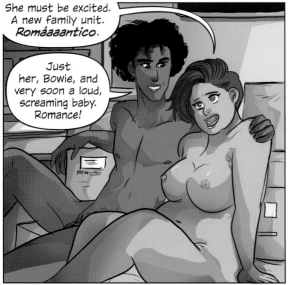

She must be excited. A new family unit. *Romáaaantico.*

Just her, Bowie, and very soon a loud, screaming baby. Romance!

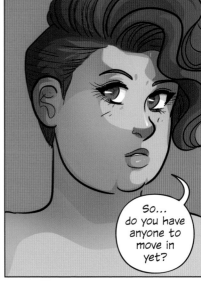

So... do you have anyone to move in yet?

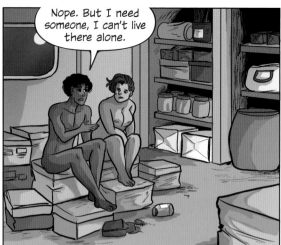

Nope. But I need someone, I can't live there alone.

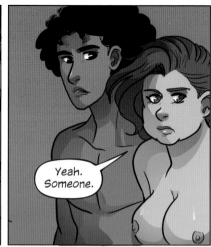

Yeah. Someone.

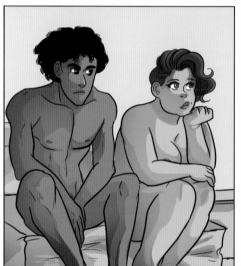

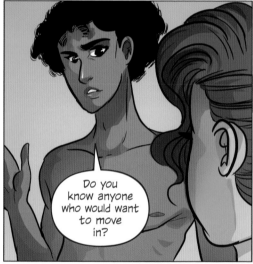

Do you know anyone who would want to move in?

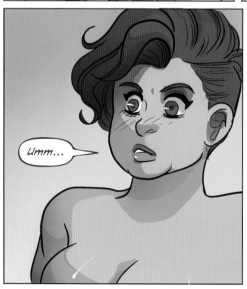

Umm...

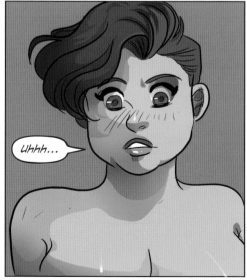

Uhhh...

Ugh. Are you two being cute?

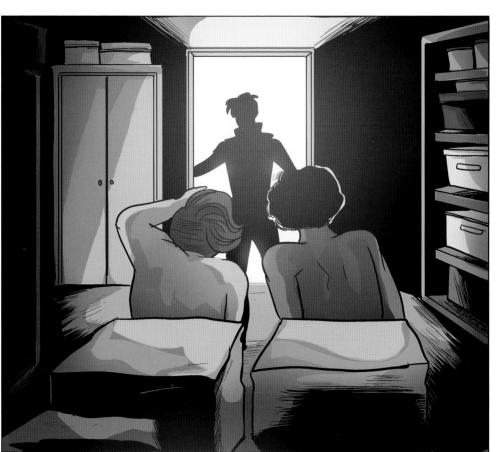

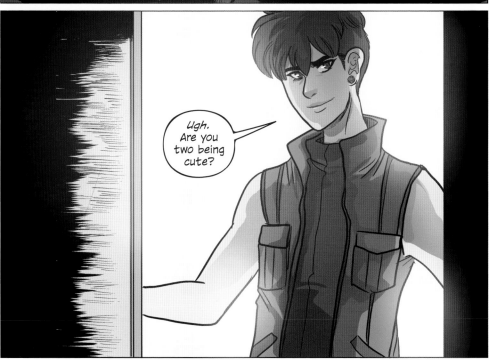

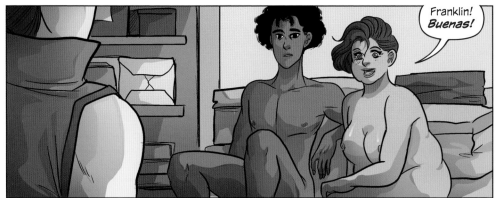

Franklin! *Buenas!*

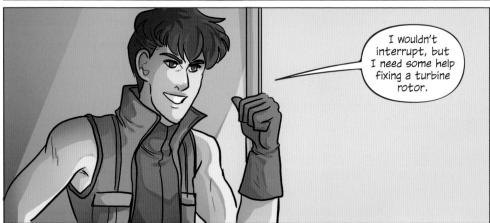

I wouldn't interrupt, but I need some help fixing a turbine rotor.

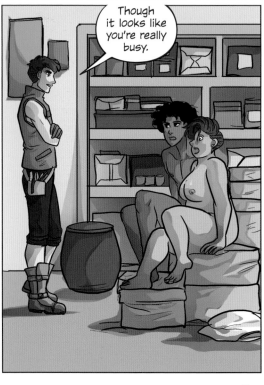

Though it looks like you're really busy.

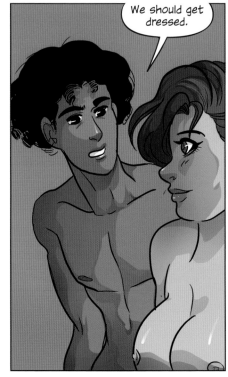

We should get dressed.

46

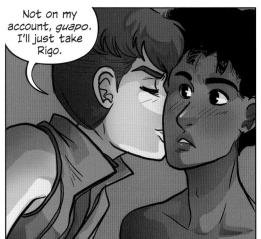

Not on my account, *guapo*. I'll just take Rigo.

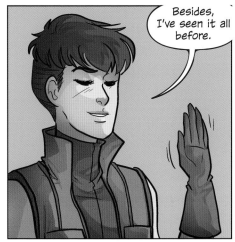

Besides, I've seen it all before.

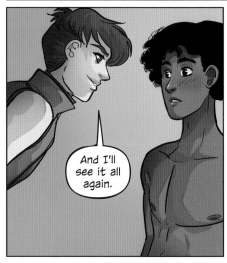

And I'll see it all again.

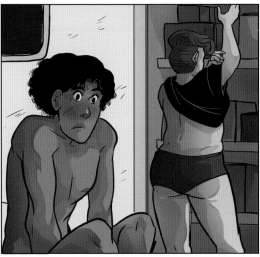

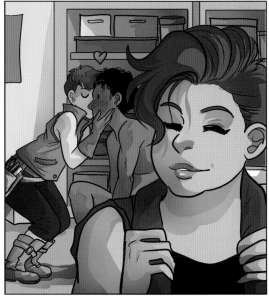

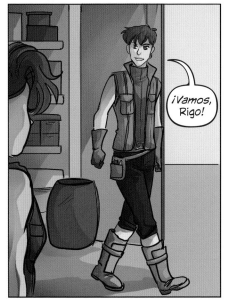

¡Vamos, Rigo!

Vrrrrrrrrr
KRRKK
Crumbs.
Here, hold this.
krrk
klak
krik
Is that safe?
No.

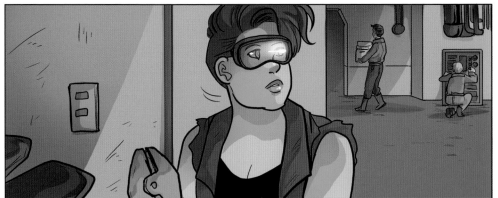

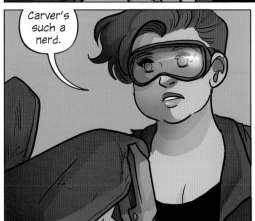

Carver's such a nerd.

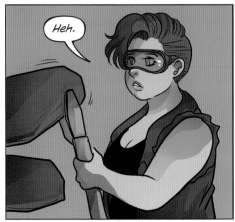

Heh.

I'm pretty sure his main turn-ons include plant genetics and spore-bearing ferns.

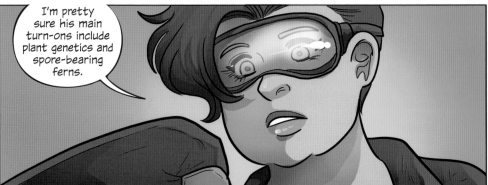

Try whispering algorithms in his ear.

Total boner.

Ha!

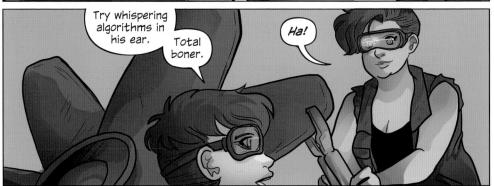

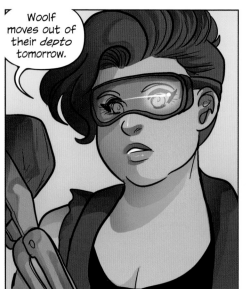

Woolf moves out of their *depto* tomorrow.

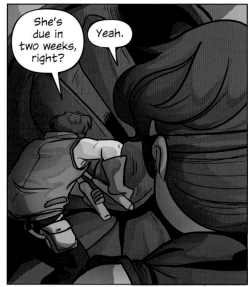

She's due in two weeks, right?

Yeah.

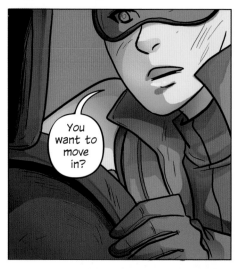

You want to move in?

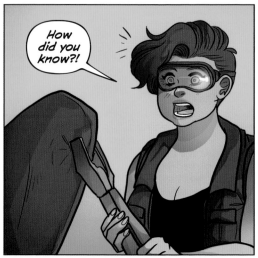

How did you know?!

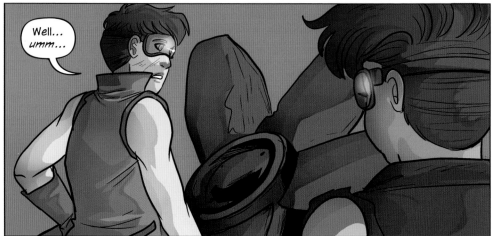

Well... umm...

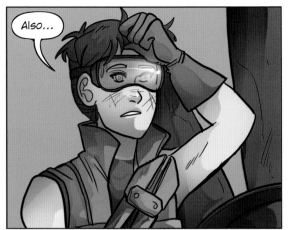

Also...

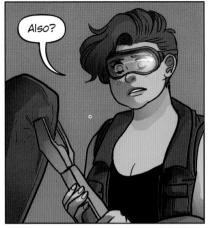

Also?

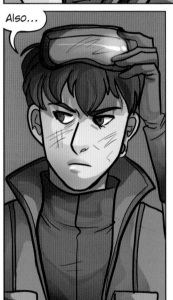

Also...

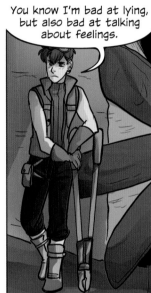

You know I'm bad at lying, but also bad at talking about feelings.

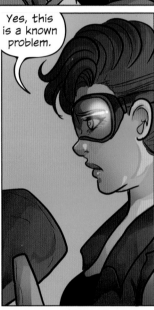

Yes, this is a known problem.

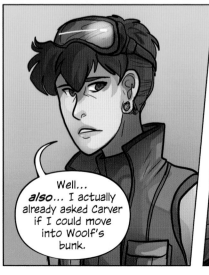

Well... *also*... I actually already asked Carver if I could move into Woolf's bunk.

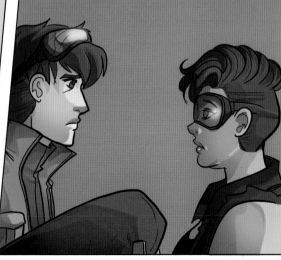

That's... fine.
Maybe it's not?
It doesn't mean anything serious, of course we can all still, you know, have sex.
Yeah, of course.
I was just thinking, practically, it would be nice to have the place.
Yeah, yeah.
It's no big deal.
Yeah, it's fine.
I can see that you're... sad? Maybe? I'm sorry?
I'm fine!
Fine!

So, what did he say?
He said he'd think about it.
I didn't think it was a big deal. Is it a big deal?
I'm just going to fix this fan...
...in utter silence...
Gracias.

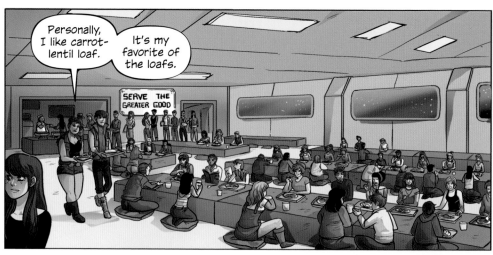

Personally, I like carrot-lentil loaf.

It's my favorite of the loafs.

SERVE THE GREATER GOOD

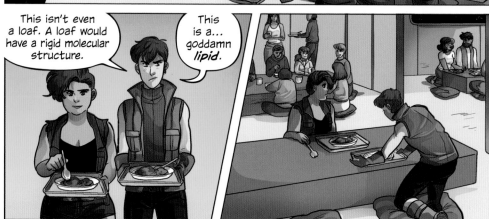

This isn't even a loaf. A loaf would have a rigid molecular structure.

This is a... goddamn *lipid*.

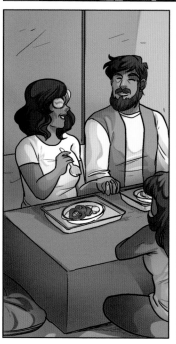

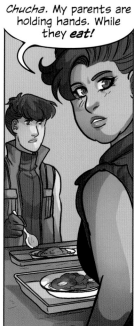

Chucha. My parents are holding hands. While they *eat!*

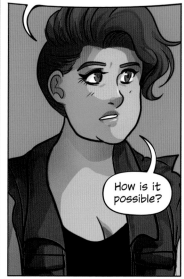

They've been with each other twenty-five years. They live in one room together. And they're still not sick of each other.

How is it possible?

Earthlings, man.
Franklin!
Did you see that hack for the moto-roto we cooked up?
Yeah! Nice work, dude!
We took the secondary arduino from the roto and...

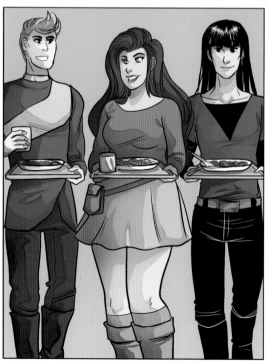

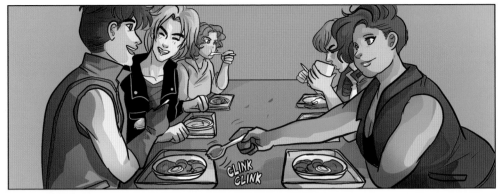

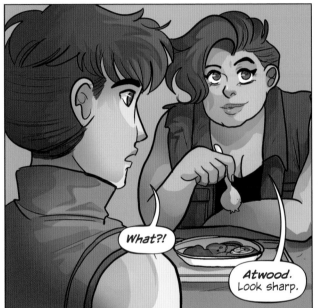

What?!

Atwood. Look sharp.

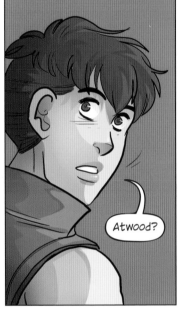

Atwood?

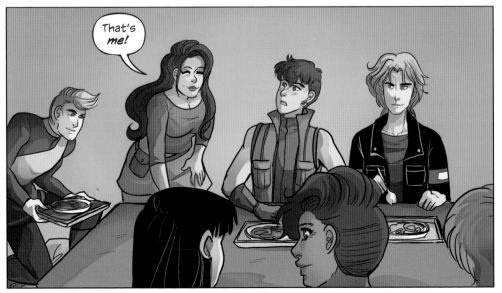

That's me!

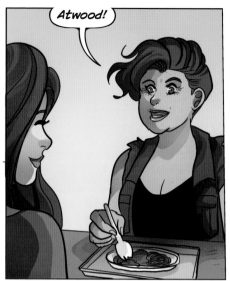

Atwood!

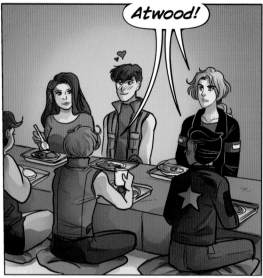

Atwood!

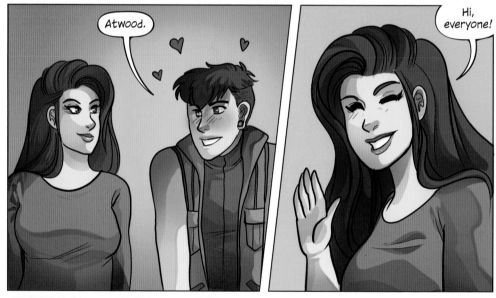

Atwood.

Hi, everyone!

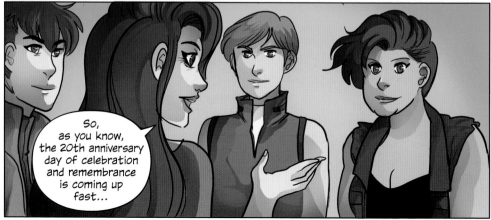

So, as you know, the 20th anniversary day of celebration and remembrance is coming up fast...

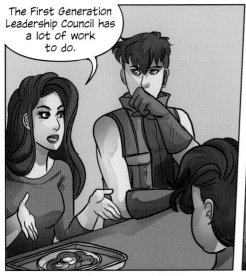

The First Generation Leadership Council has a lot of work to do.

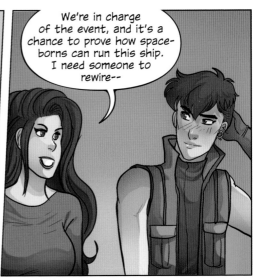

We're in charge of the event, and it's a chance to prove how space-borns can run this ship. I need someone to rewire--

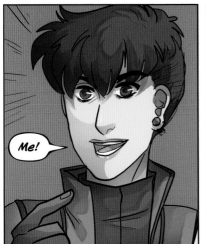

Me!

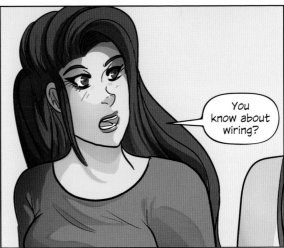

You know about wiring?

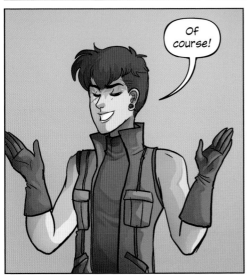

Of course!

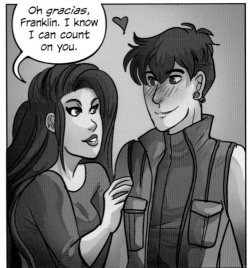

Oh *gracias*, Franklin. I know I can count on you.

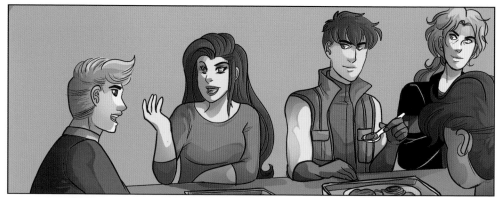

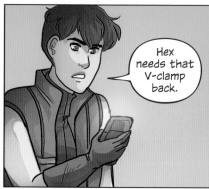

Hex needs that V-clamp back.

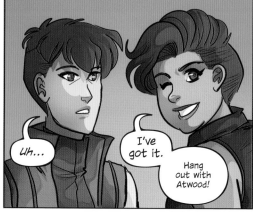

BRZT

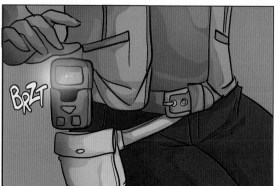

¡Quédate aquí! I'll go deliver it.

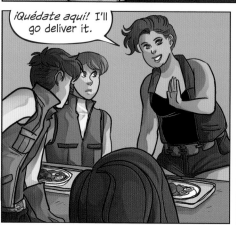

Uh...

I've got it.

Hang out with Atwood!

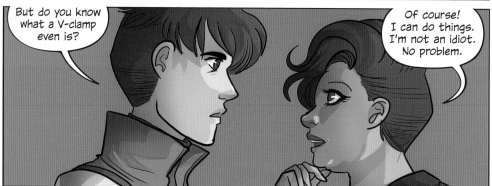

But do you know what a V-clamp even is?

Of course! I can do things. I'm not an idiot. No problem.

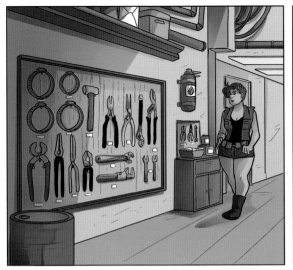

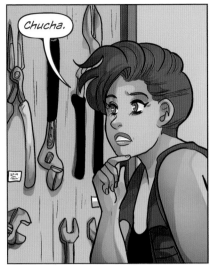

Chucha.

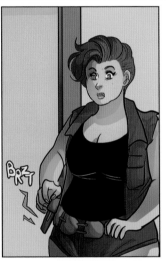

BRT

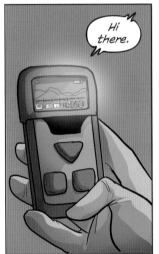

Hi there.

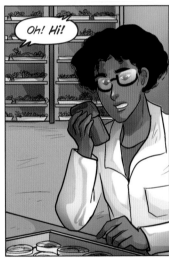

Oh! Hi!

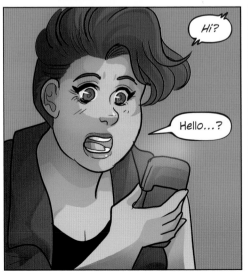

Hi?

Hello...?

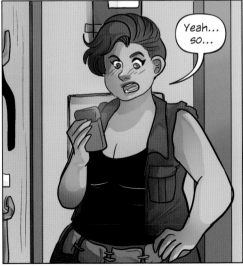

Yeah... so...

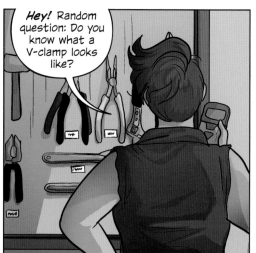

Hey! Random question: Do you know what a V-clamp looks like?

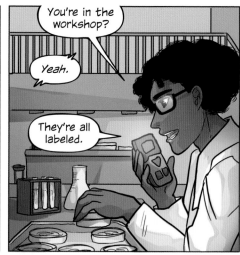

You're in the workshop?

Yeah.

They're all labeled.

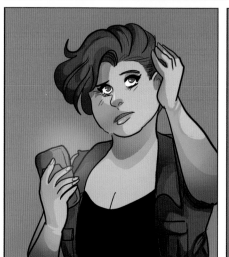

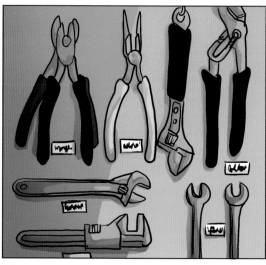

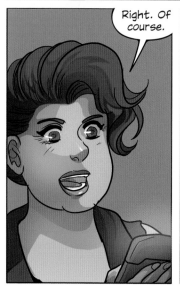

Right. Of course.

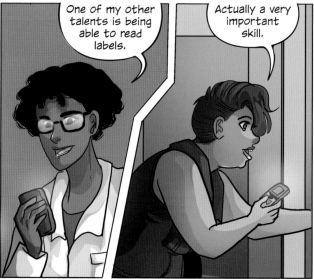

One of my other talents is being able to read labels.

Actually a very important skill.

So... *uh*... how about lunch today? Gross, right?
Um, I think it was fine?
Ha! *Yeah. I guess. So...*
This morning was nice.
It's always nice.
Are you busy tonight?
20:00
21:00
22:00
SARAH
RIGO
CARVER
ARI
RIGO
Me? You want to hang out with ***me?***

I'm done at 22 hundred.
Cool.
So... I'll come by the farm? We can hang out?
Yeah. You okay?
I'm great!!
Okay, great!
Great! Bye!

Oh, hey.

Helloooo.
Did you bring that V-clamp?
One V-clamp, right here!
Yes, exactly, *that* is what I'm here for!
Gracias, babe.
De nada.

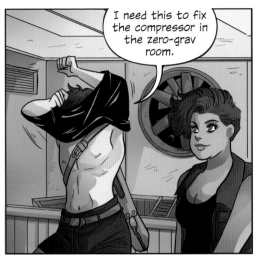

I need this to fix the compressor in the zero-grav room.

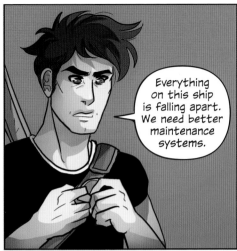

Everything on this ship is falling apart. We need better maintenance systems.

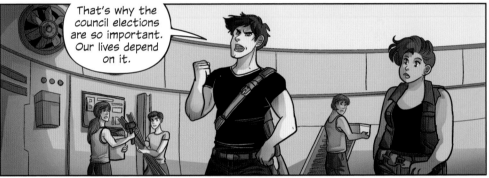

That's why the council elections are so important. Our lives depend on it.

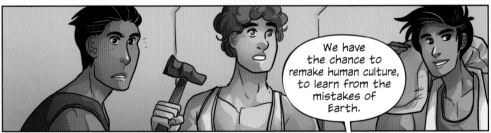

We have the chance to remake human culture, to learn from the mistakes of Earth.

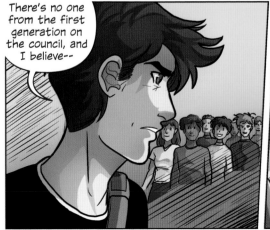

There's no one from the first generation on the council, and I believe--

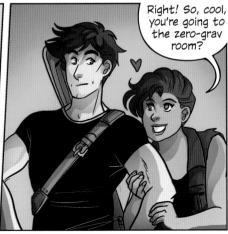

Right! So, cool, you're going to the zero-grav room?

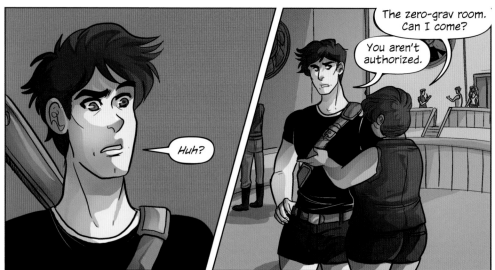

Huh?

The zero-grav room. Can I come?

You aren't authorized.

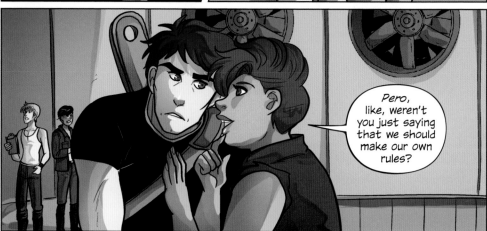

Pero, like, weren't you just saying that we should make our own rules?

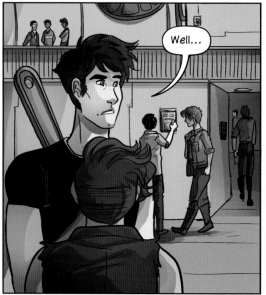

Well...

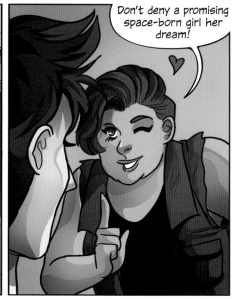

Don't deny a promising space-born girl her dream!

You have a dream of training to be part of the space-walk team?
No, Hex, I have a dream of having sex with you in zero G.
Oh!
It's the only place on this *chingado* Earth heap with any privacy.
!!!
Vamos!

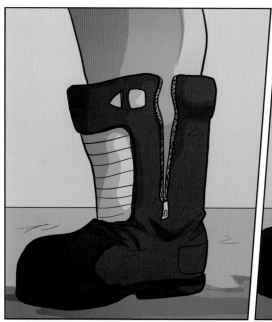

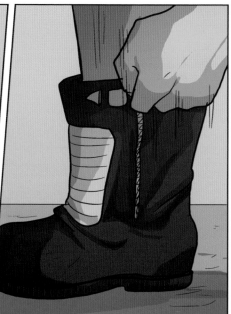

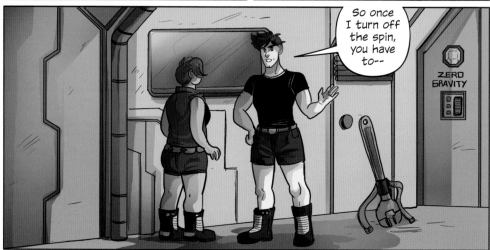

So once I turn off the spin, you have to--

ZERO GRAVITY

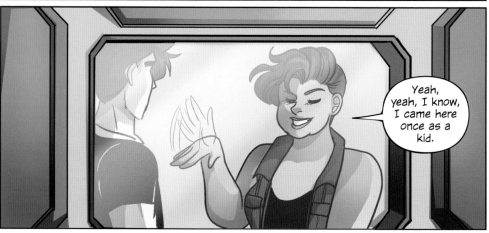

Yeah, yeah, I know, I came here once as a kid.

Just be careful.
I know what I'm doing.
You don't have to be such a--
¡Chucha!
ZERO GRAV ROOM

ZERO
GRAV
ROOM

You good?
Very.
ROOM
Still good?
Very, ***very*** good.

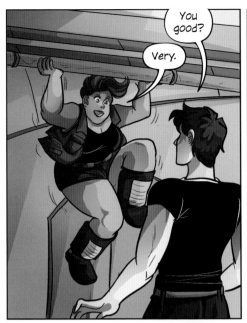

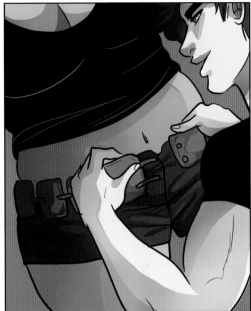

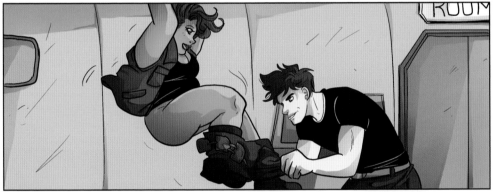

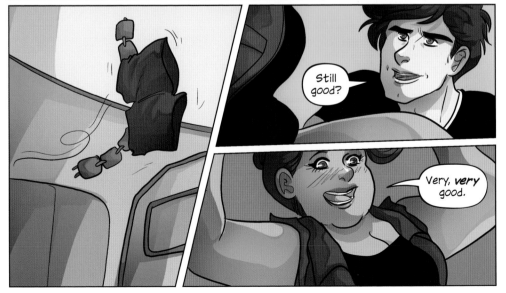

Gah!
So goddamn good.
Aaaaaah!
Don't lose your grip.

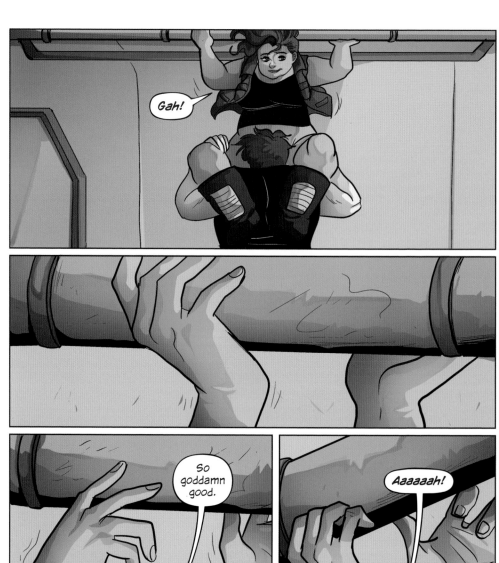

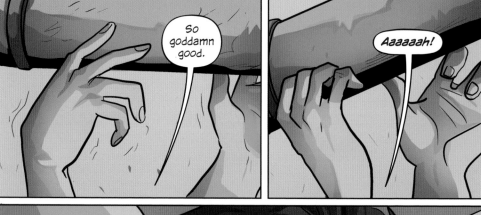

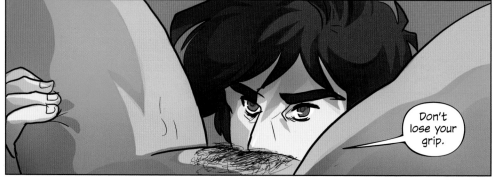

Ah!
¡Chucha!

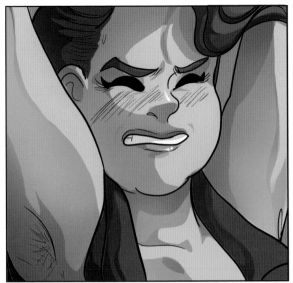

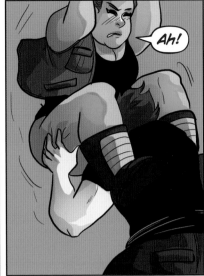

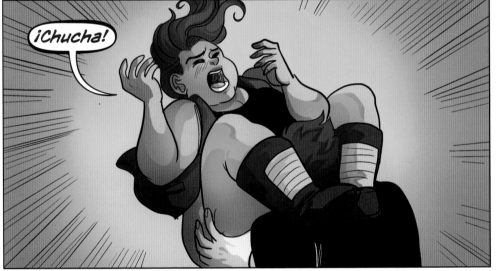

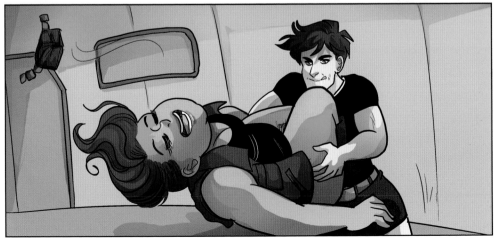

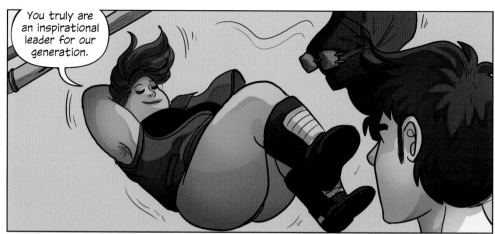

You truly are an inspirational leader for our generation.

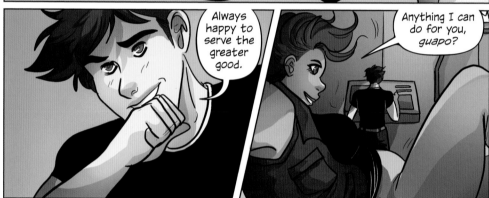

Always happy to serve the greater good.

Anything I can do for you, *guapo*?

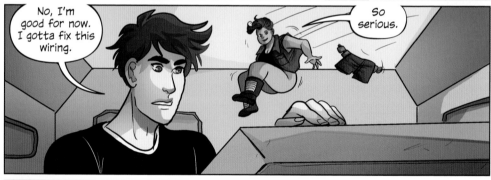

No, I'm good for now. I gotta fix this wiring.

So serious.

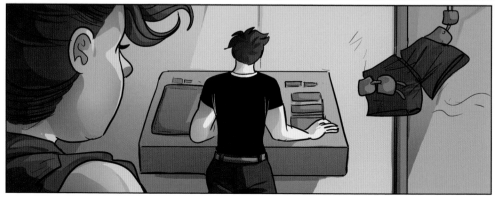

Hex?

Hm?

You ever think about partnering up someday?

Are you proposing?

No! Ha, no.

I mean, you're great, though!

Of course I do.

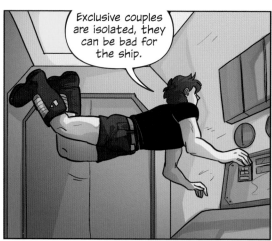

Exclusive couples are isolated, they can be bad for the ship.

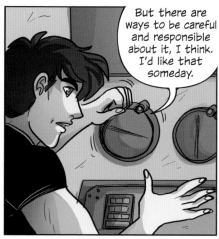

But there are ways to be careful and responsible about it, I think. I'd like that someday.

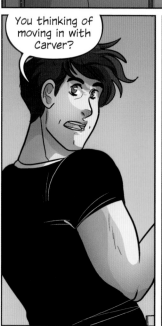

You thinking of moving in with Carver?

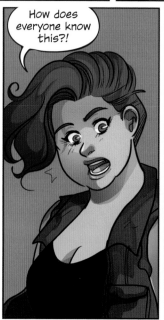

How does everyone know this?!

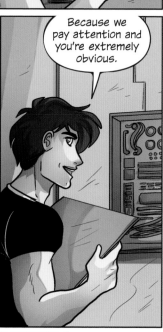

Because we pay attention and you're extremely obvious.

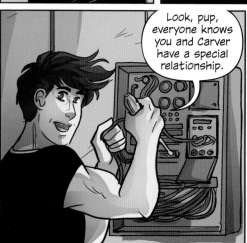

Look, pup, everyone knows you and Carver have a special relationship.

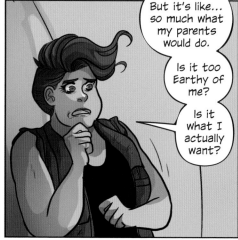

But it's like... so much what my parents would do.

Is it too Earthy of me?

Is it what I actually want?

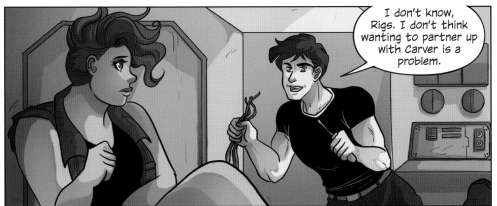

I don't know, Rigs. I don't think wanting to partner up with Carver is a problem.

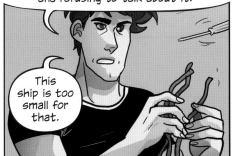

Unless you make it one by getting all weird and refusing to talk about it.

This ship is too small for that.

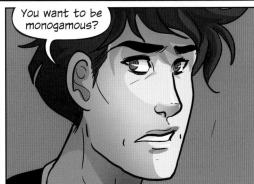

You want to be monogamous?

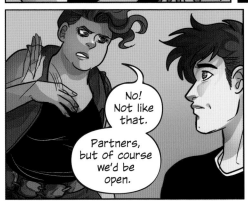

No! Not like that.

Partners, but of course we'd be open.

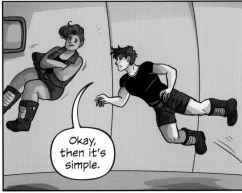

Okay, then it's simple.

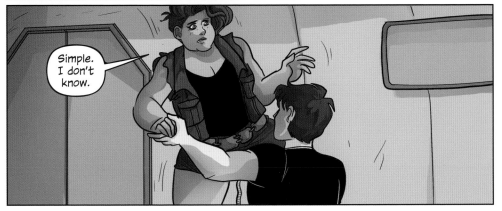

Simple. I don't know.

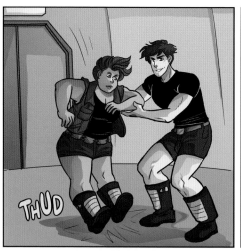

THUD

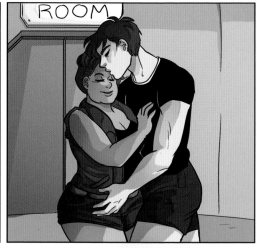

ROOM

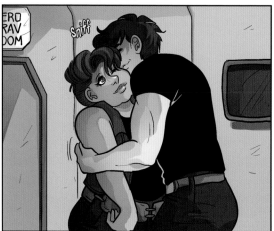

Sniff

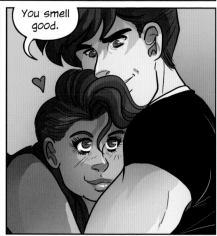

You smell good.

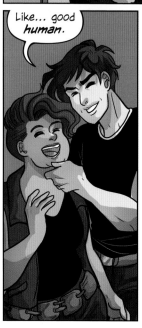

Like... good **human.**

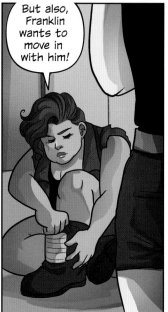

But also, Franklin wants to move in with him!

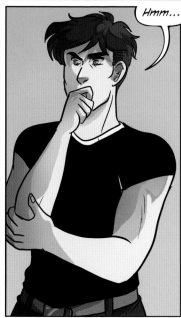

Hmm...

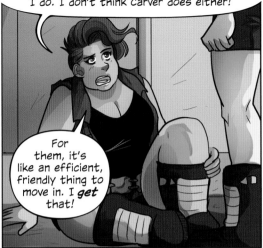

Of course Franks and Carver also get sexy, but I don't think Franks wants to partner up like I do. I don't think Carver does either!

For them, it's like an efficient, friendly thing to move in. I **get** that!

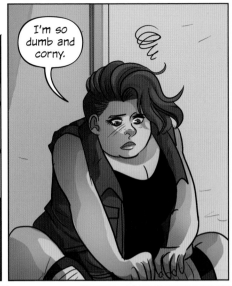

I'm so dumb and corny.

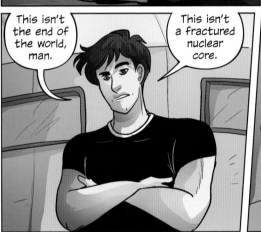

This isn't the end of the world, man.

This isn't a fractured nuclear core.

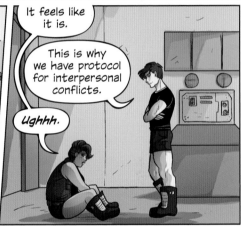

It feels like it is.

This is why we have protocol for interpersonal conflicts.

Ughhh.

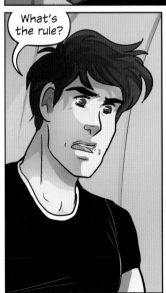

What's the rule?

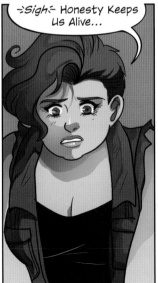

⊰*Sigh*⊱ Honesty Keeps Us Alive...

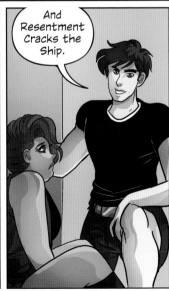

And Resentment Cracks the Ship.

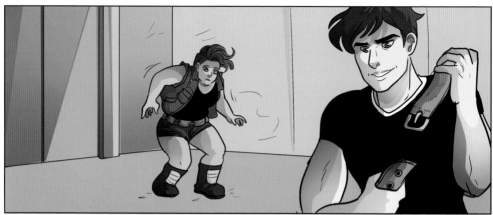

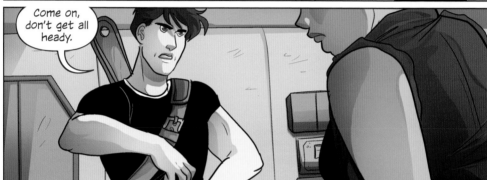

Come on, don't get all heady.

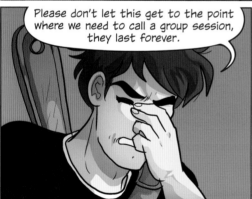

Please don't let this get to the point where we need to call a group session, they last forever.

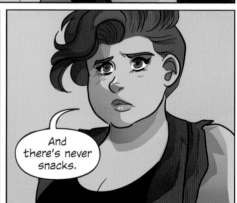

And there's never snacks.

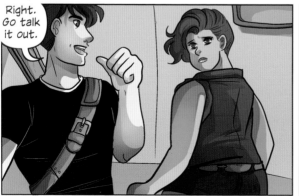

Right. Go talk it out.

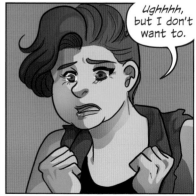

Ughhhh, but I don't want to.

Oooo...
Mmmmm...
Oh!
Oh!
ymmrkgoorkd
What?

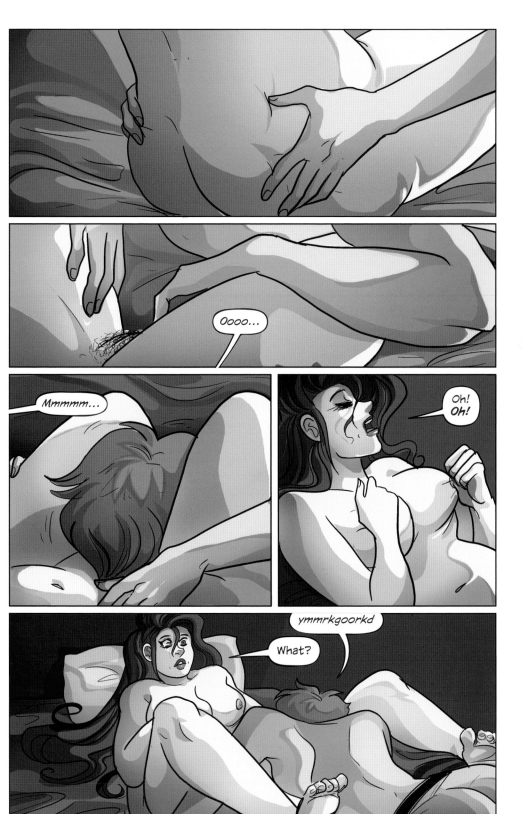

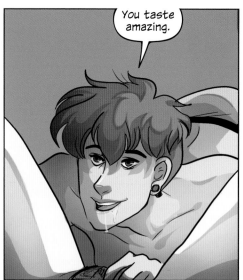

You taste amazing.

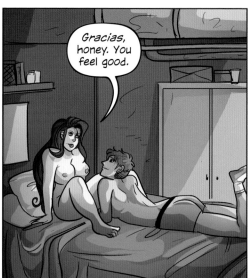

Gracias, honey. You feel good.

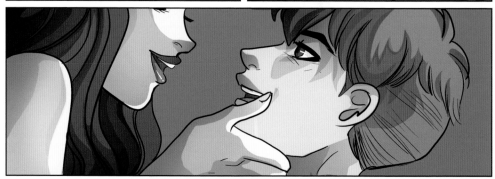

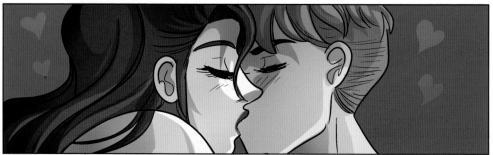

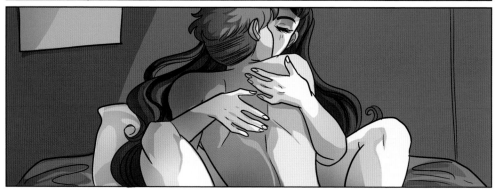

Heeeeey.
You like that?
Yes, ma'am.
You want more?
Yes, please, ma'am.
Franklin!

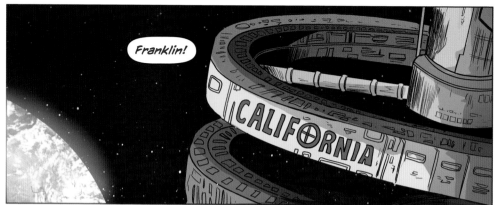

Franklin!

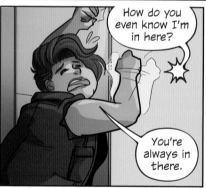

They say in space, no one can hear you scream.

Frankliiiiin!

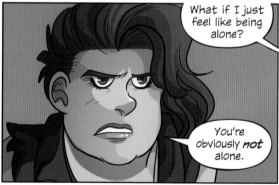

I enjoy proving them wrong whenever possible.

Fraaaaanks, I am going to die if you don't open this door.

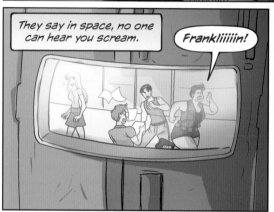

How do you even know I'm in here?

You're always in there.

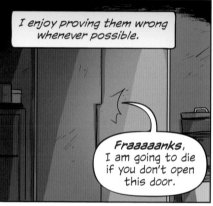

What if I just feel like being alone?

You're obviously *not* alone.

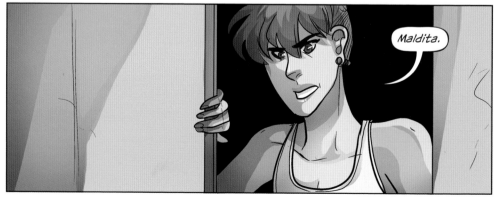

Maldita.

Hi, Rigo.
What do you want?
I wanted to come talk.
What's wrong, sweets?

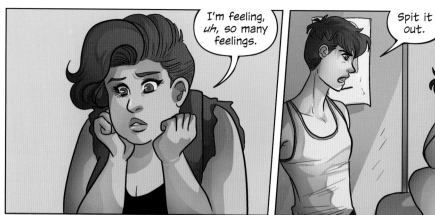

I'm feeling, *uh*, so many feelings.

Spit it out.

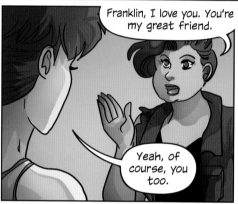

Franklin, I love you. You're my great friend.

Yeah, of course, you too.

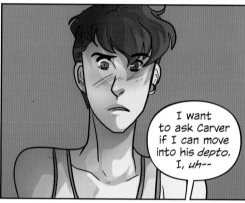

I want to ask Carver if I can move into his *depto*. I, *uh*--

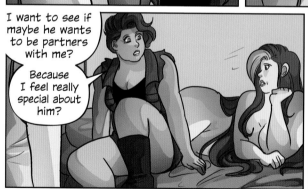

I want to see if maybe he wants to be partners with me?

Because I feel really special about him?

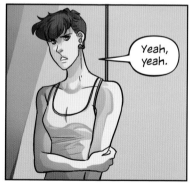

Yeah, yeah.

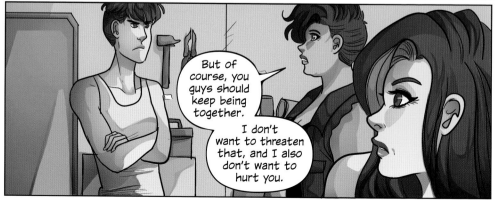

But of course, you guys should keep being together.

I don't want to threaten that, and I also don't want to hurt you.

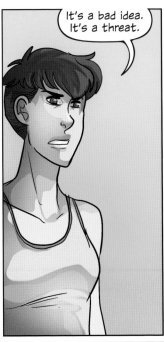

It's a bad idea. It's a threat.

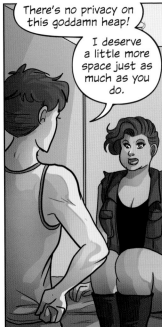

There's no privacy on this goddamn heap!

I deserve a little more space just as much as you do.

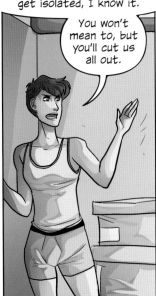

If you move in, you two are going to be all in love and get isolated, I know it.

You won't mean to, but you'll cut us all out.

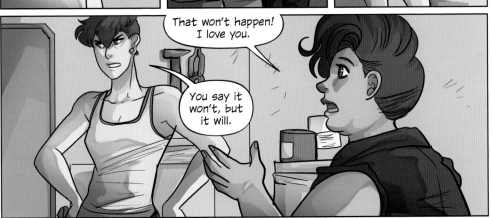

That won't happen! I love you.

You say it won't, but it will.

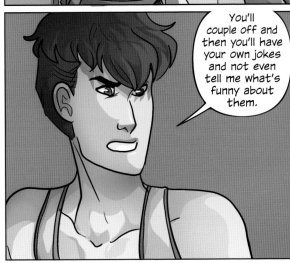

You'll couple off and then you'll have your own jokes and not even tell me what's funny about them.

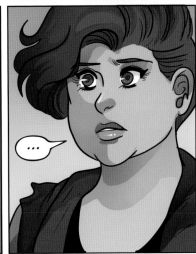

...

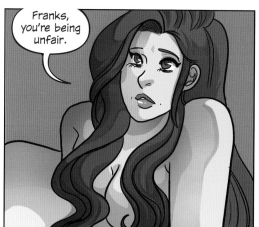

Franks, you're being unfair.

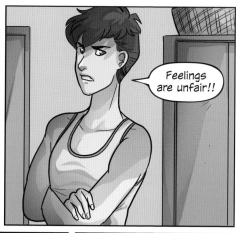

Feelings are unfair!!

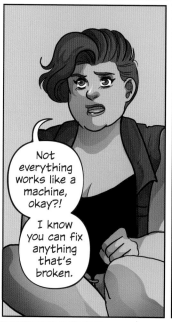

Not everything works like a machine, okay?!

I know you can fix anything that's broken.

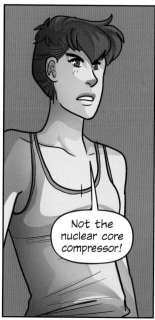

Not the nuclear core compressor!

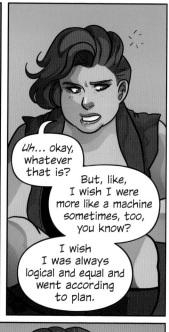

Uh... okay, whatever that is?

But, like, I wish I were more like a machine sometimes, too, you know?

I wish I was always logical and equal and went according to plan.

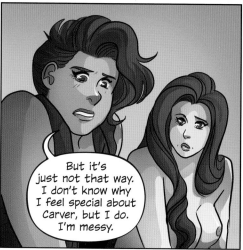

But it's just not that way. I don't know why I feel special about Carver, but I do. I'm messy.

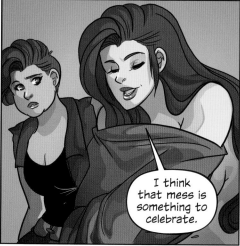

I think that mess is something to celebrate.

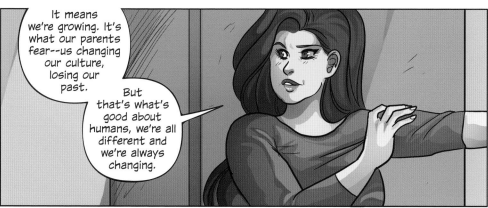

It means we're growing. It's what our parents fear--us changing our culture, losing our past.

But that's what's good about humans, we're all different and we're always changing.

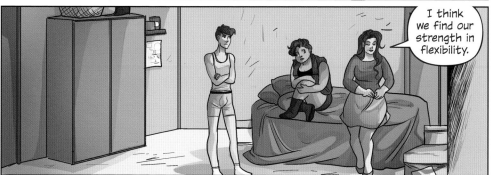

I think we find our strength in flexibility.

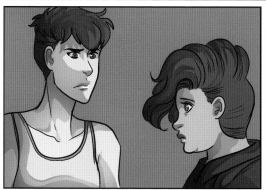

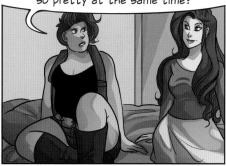

Atwood, how are you both so smart and so pretty at the same time?

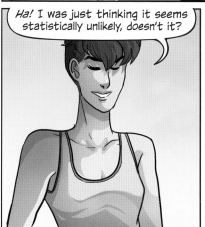

Ha! I was just thinking it seems statistically unlikely, doesn't it?

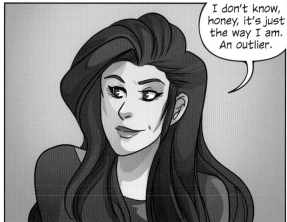

I don't know, honey, it's just the way I am. An outlier.

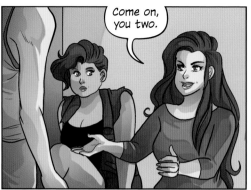

Come on, you two.

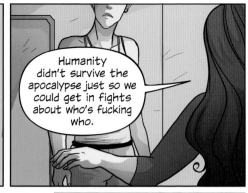

Humanity didn't survive the apocalypse just so we could get in fights about who's fucking who.

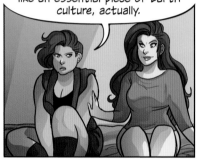

Are you sure? Because that seems like an essential piece of Earth culture, actually.

We're the first generation. We get to decide what to take and leave.

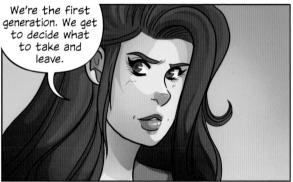

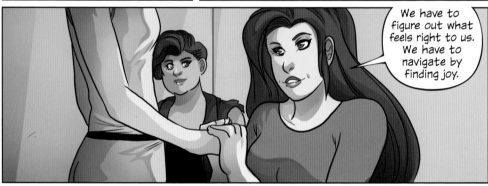

We have to figure out what feels right to us. We have to navigate by finding joy.

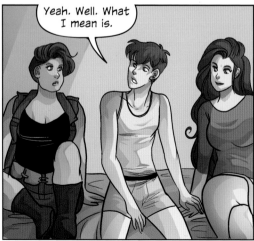

Yeah. Well. What I mean is.

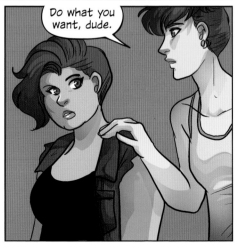

Do what you want, dude.

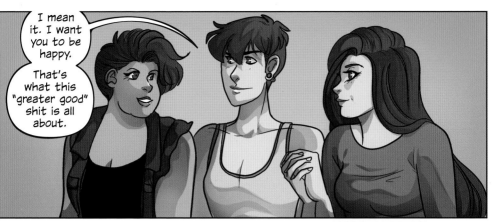

I mean it. I want you to be happy.

That's what this "greater good" shit is all about.

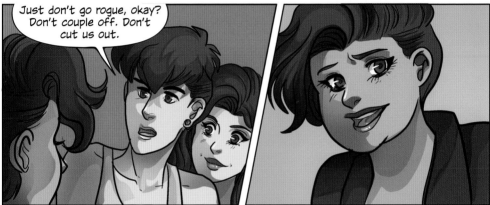

Just don't go rogue, okay? Don't couple off. Don't cut us out.

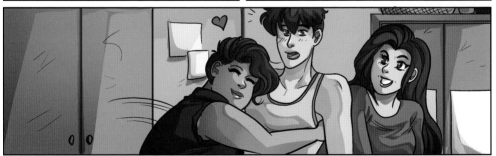

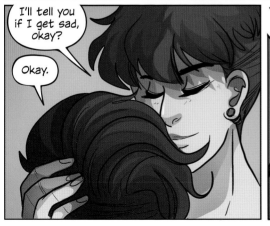

I'll tell you if I get sad, okay?

Okay.

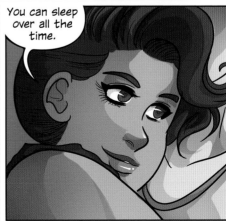

You can sleep over all the time.

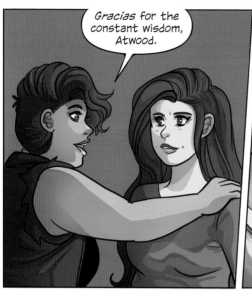
Gracias for the constant wisdom, Atwood.

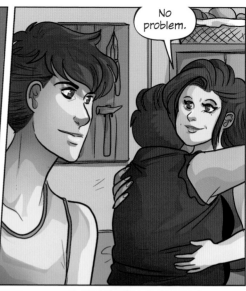
No problem.

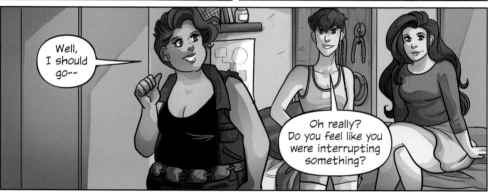
Well, I should go--

Oh really? Do you feel like you were interrupting something?

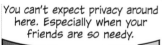
You can't expect privacy around here. Especially when your friends are so needy.

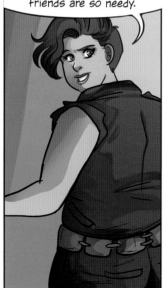

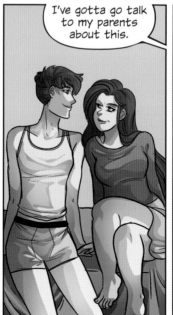
I've gotta go talk to my parents about this.

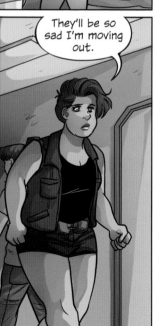
They'll be so sad I'm moving out.

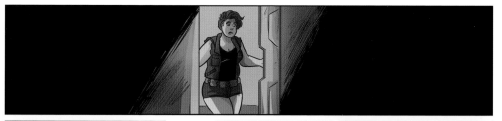

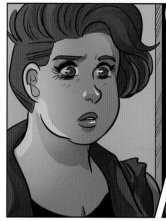

¿Mami?
¿Papi?

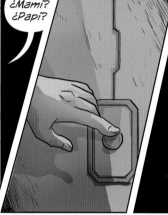

Don't turn on the light!

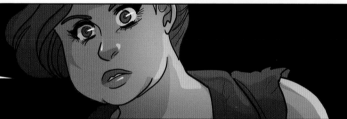

What? Why not? Why do you guys have the lights off?

Asleep? It's barely past dinner.

I have a headache.

I'm asleep.

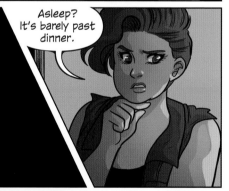

Uh... It's been a long day.

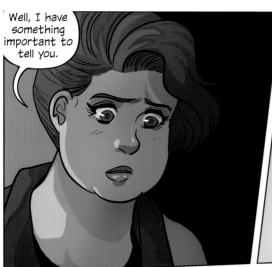

Well, I have something important to tell you.

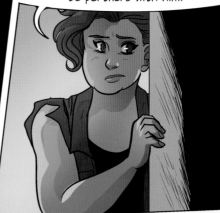

I'm going to ask Carver if I can move into his family's *depto.* I'm going to be partners with him.

¡Qué bueno!

That's great, dear!

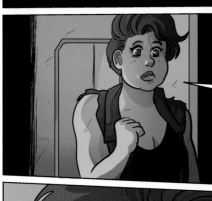

Yeah?

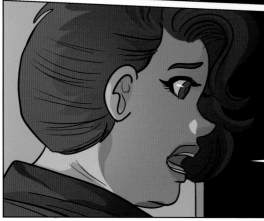

I thought you guys might be sad.

It means I'm moving out.

Ah, yes, very sad!

But we want you to be happy!

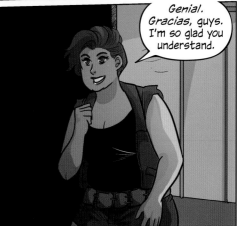

Genial. Gracias, guys. I'm so glad you understand.

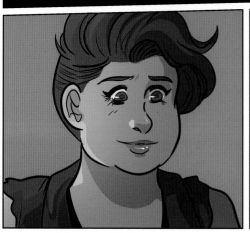

Okay, ¡buenas noches! ¡Te amo!

¡Buenas noches!

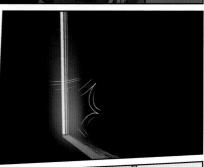

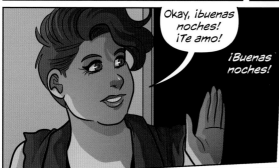

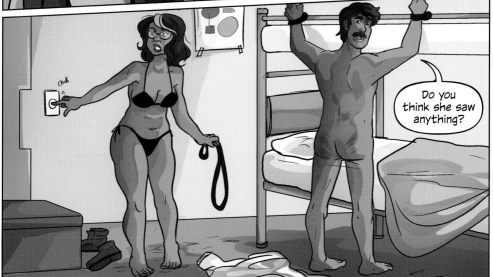

Click

Do you think she saw anything?

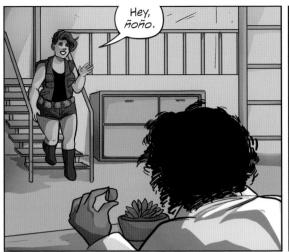

Hey, ñoño.

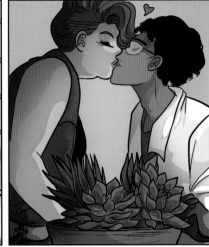

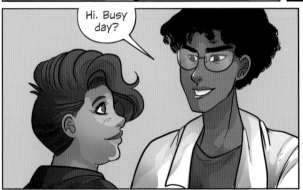

Hi. Busy day?

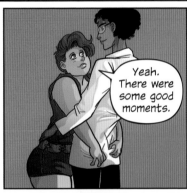

Yeah. There were some good moments.

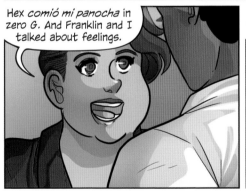

Hex *comió mi panocha* in zero G. And Franklin and I talked about feelings.

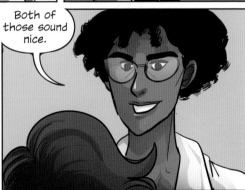

Both of those sound nice.

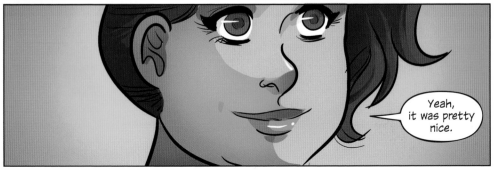

Yeah, it was pretty nice.

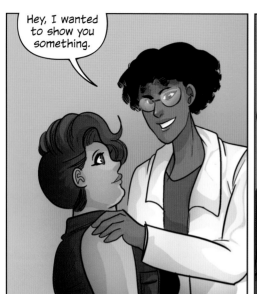

Hey, I wanted to show you something.

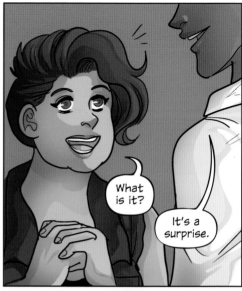

What is it?

It's a surprise.

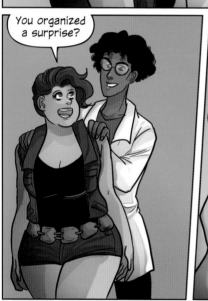

You organized a surprise?

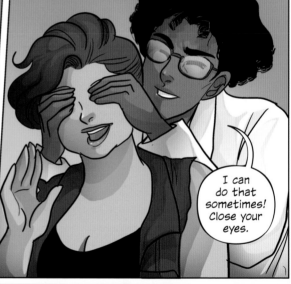

I can do that sometimes! Close your eyes.

Can I open them now?
No.
I'm going to run into a wall.
No, you're not.
Okay, this is a door, walk through it.
Oh! It's your *depto.*
I was wondering if you'd like to make it yours, too.

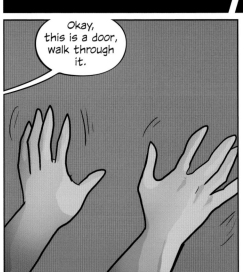

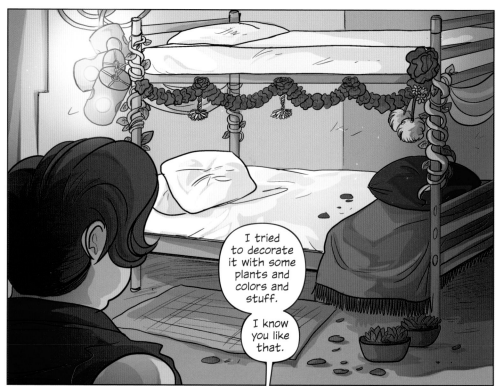

I tried to decorate it with some plants and colors and stuff.

I know you like that.

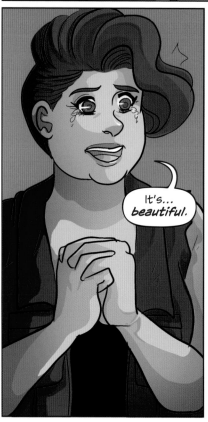

It's... *beautiful.*

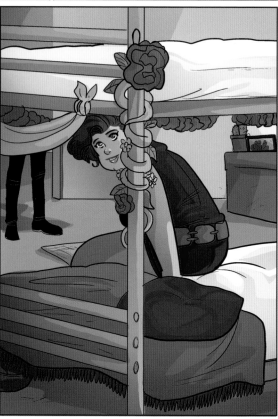

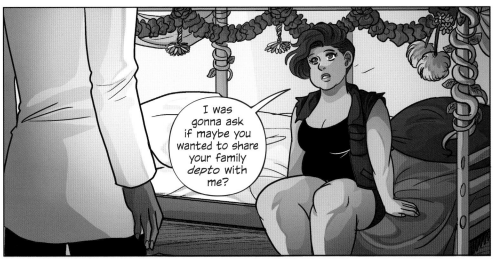

I was gonna ask if maybe you wanted to share your family *depto* with me?

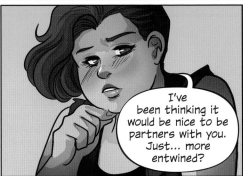

I've been thinking it would be nice to be partners with you. Just... more entwined?

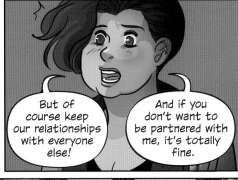

But of course keep our relationships with everyone else!

And if you don't want to be partnered with me, it's totally fine.

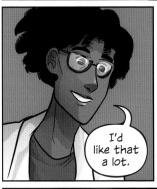

I'd like that a lot.

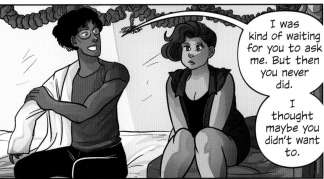

I was kind of waiting for you to ask me. But then you never did.

I thought maybe you didn't want to.

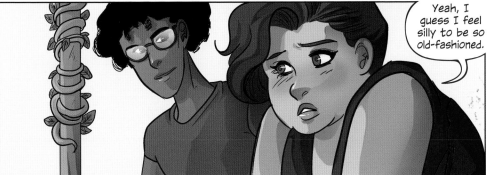

Yeah, I guess I feel silly to be so old-fashioned.

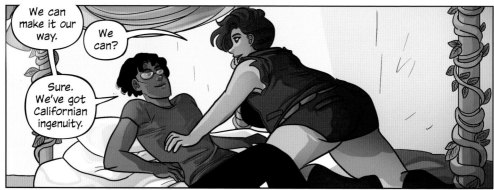

We can make it our way.

We can?

Sure. We've got Californian ingenuity.

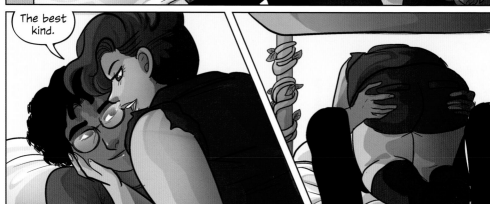

The best kind.

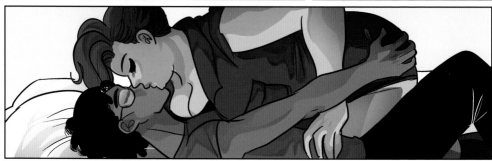

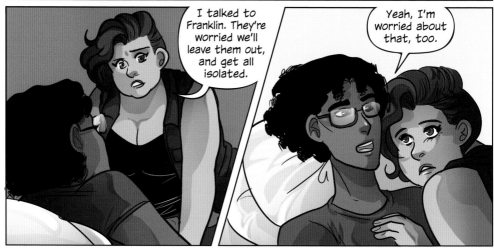

I talked to Franklin. They're worried we'll leave them out, and get all isolated.

Yeah, I'm worried about that, too.

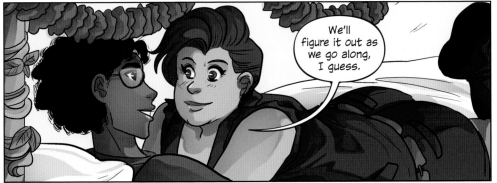

We'll figure it out as we go along, I guess.

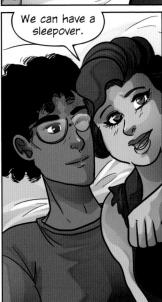

We can have a sleepover.

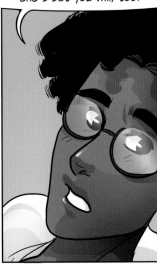

Yeah, I'll want some alone time with them sometimes, and I bet you will, too.

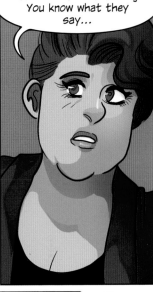

Yeah. We'll talk it through. You know what they say...

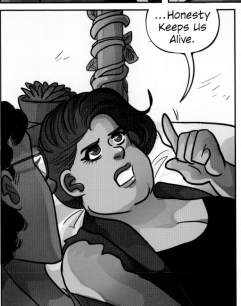

...Honesty Keeps Us Alive.

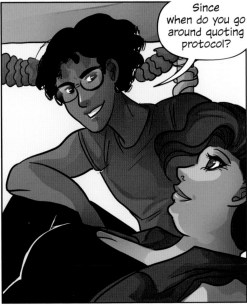

Since when do you go around quoting protocol?

Since I spend too much time hanging out with Hex.

Oh yeah? What else did that civic leader teach you?

Hey!

Ack! You got my glasses all steamy.

Pobresito ñoño.

Ack.
Can I get my hands back?
No.
Wait, isn't your sister still in here?

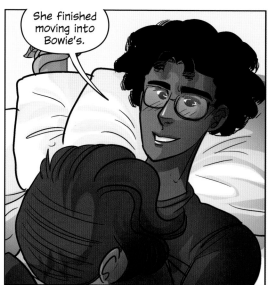

She finished moving into Bowie's.

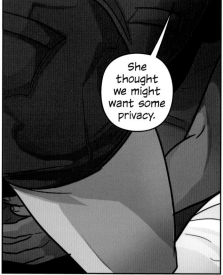

She thought we might want some privacy.

She's so nice.

You are also very nice.

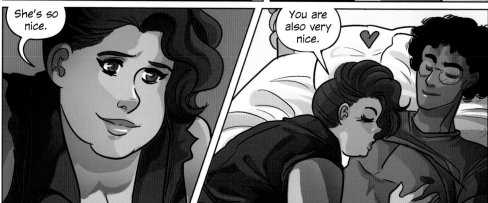

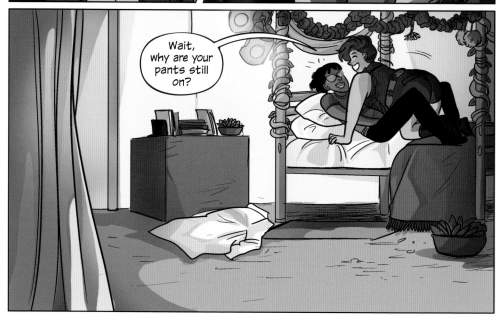

Wait, why are your pants still on?

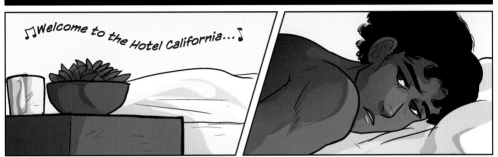

♫Welcome to the Hotel California...♪

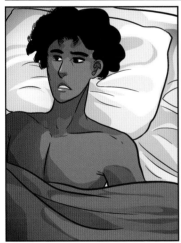

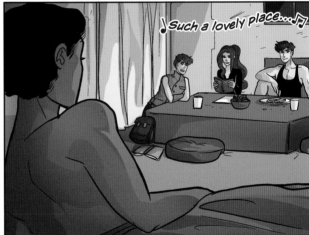

♪Such a lovely place...♫♪

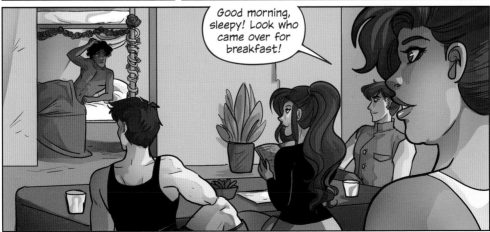

Good morning, sleepy! Look who came over for breakfast!

Are you going to sing that terrible song every morning?
I hope so.
It sounds better than your snoring, at least.
I wasn't snoring.
You were snoring.
This is so unfair, I'm going back to sleep.

Let us at least get earplugs first, honey.
Or we can eject him in the evacuation capsule, maybe.
You're so mean, just leave me alone.
Never.
CALIFORNIA
Just another beautiful day in California.

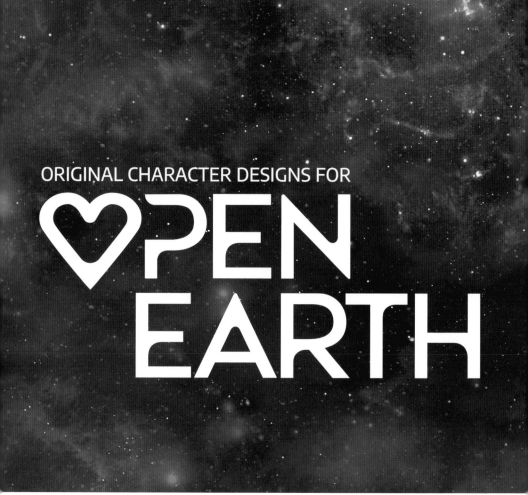

ORIGINAL CHARACTER DESIGNS FOR

OPEN EARTH

RIGO

SARAH MIRK: For me, it was important to have Rigo depicted as a short, curvy girl who's confident in her body. She has grown up in a culture that's different than ours on Earth—there's no pop culture, no consumerism, no industry that's geared around telling her she needs to look a very specific way in order to be pretty. She loves her body because it's strong, soft, and brings her a lot of pleasure.

EVA CABRERA: What I wanted for Rigo was to show her feelings and her funny personality through her expressiveness. I especially focused on her face for this. I love that she's funny, adorable and full of love.

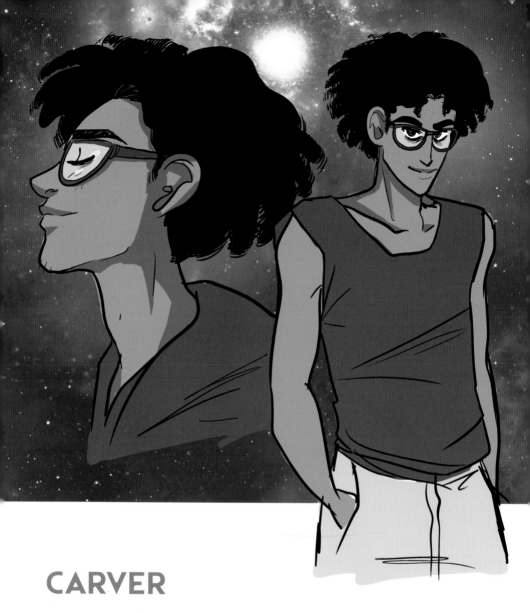

CARVER

SARAH MIRK: I love seeing the way Carver looks when put into awkward situations. I imagined him as an adorable nerd, someone who's very sweet and romantic at heart, but also approaches relationships from a practical standpoint: we should do what feels good, right? It's just logical.

EVA CABRERA: Carver was very easy to draw. He's a simple, sensitive guy and his style just popped into my head! I love his relationship with Rigo, a classic shy guy with a loud, boisterous girl.

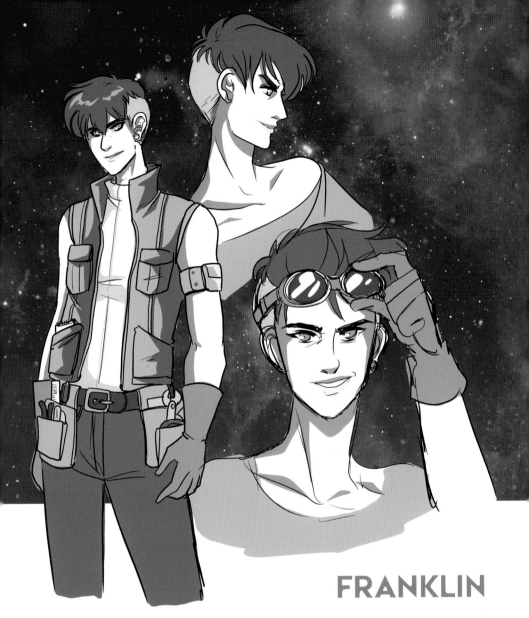

FRANKLIN

SARAH MIRK: I often wonder about how young people will think about their own gender in the future. I hope that the increasing freedom people have now to dress and define themselves however they want will expand more and more, to the point where it's completely accepted for people to be non-binary, like Franklin. Franklin is a quiet person who prefers tinkering with machines to talking to humans, but I wanted it to be clear from the way they carry themselves that they are deeply confident and capable.

EVA CABRERA: I just LOVE Franklin! Franklin has a great style and is cool in the face of danger. I wanted to channel that through their demeanor, and of course, I love their little screw-earring.

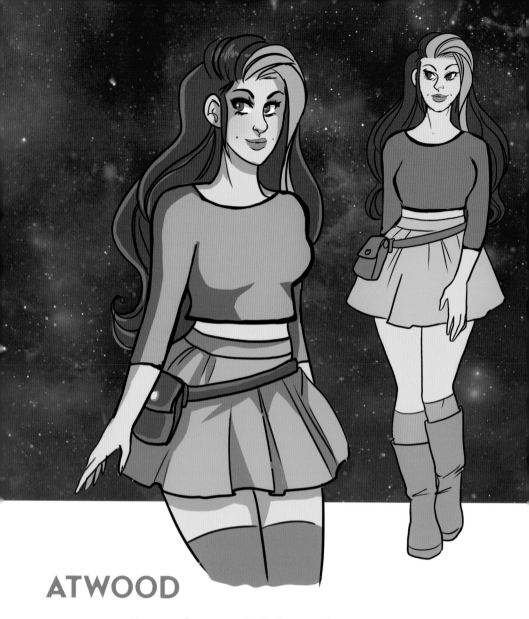

ATWOOD

SARAH MIRK: Femmes forever! I think that in a future where people express gender in a more dynamic way, there will still be people who identify as femmes. Atwood is sexy because she knows what she likes and she loves being sensual.

EVA CABRERA: My favorite femme to draw! I wanted to make her stand out from other characters. With her curviness, her intelligence and her patience, she's probably my favorite character.

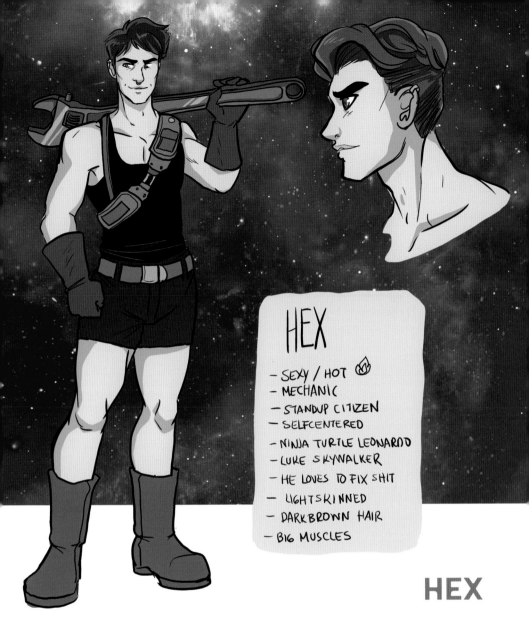

HEX

- SEXY / HOT 🔥
- MECHANIC
- STANDUP CITIZEN
- SELFCENTERED
- NINJA TURTLE LEONARDO
- LUKE SKYWALKER
- HE LOVES TO FIX SHIT
- LIGHTSKINNED
- DARKBROWN HAIR
- BIG MUSCLES

HEX

SARAH MIRK: For me, the most important part of Hex's character design was his short shorts. I love me some guy-thigh. Plus, longer pants are impractical—Hex is a mechanic who likes getting down into the heart of the *California*'s engines. His days are filled with grease and sweat, of course he needs tiny shorts to keep himself cool. I wanted his giant wrench to look like something that would show up in a *Final Fantasy* game. I think Eva really nailed the design, all around.

EVA CABRERA: Hex was super fun to design. He's sexy but at the same time someone who would listen and give you great advice like he does with Rigo. I love getting involved with the characters I draw, and in him I wanted to portray a buff, kind man with hot shorts.

ACKNOWLEDGEMENTS

Thanks to Raqui, Daniel, Adam, and Julia for not laughing at the idea for this book, and instead encouraging me to make it a reality. Thanks to my partner Ben and my friend Becky for talking with me about queerness. Thanks to Joe Mar for reading over the first draft, and to Noah and Merle in Berlin for letting me stay with them while I wrote the second draft. I'm so impressed with Eva and Claudia's amazing character design and brilliant colors—thank you two! I feel deep gratitude to editor Ari Yarwood for shepherding this funny little book along, and checking every detail—every writer in the world could use an editor as diligent as her. —SARAH MIRK

I want to thank my team: Sarah, Claudia and Ari, it was very cool to work with you. (Thank you very much Ari for the vegetarian food, I loved meeting you in person and having a good time.) To Limerence Press for this opportunity and their attention, I love you and I hope in the future to return to work with you. It has been a great year and an experience that I will never forget.
—EVA CABRERA

It's been an honor to work with these kind and talented humans. Thank you Ari, Sarah, Eva. I want to thank Diana Camero for her infinite patience and support during this project, and Rina for her help with flats. You've all been amazing, and it's been a wonderful experience I'd love to repeat. And of course, I'd love to thank Limerence Press for the chance to make it possible in the first place. You rock! —CLAUDIA AGUIRRE

BIOGRAPHIES

SARAH MIRK is the author of the modern relationship guidebook *Sex from Scratch: Making Your Own Relationship Rules* and is the former online editor of feminism and pop culture nonprofit Bitch Media. She's now a contributing editor at graphic journalism site The Nib, where she writes nonfiction comics about everything from mansplaining to monogamy.

mirkwork.com / @sarahmirk

EVA CABRERA is a Latina traveler and comic book artist of *Open Earth* from Limerence Press, *Betty & Veronica: Vixens* from Archie Comics, and the Eisner-nominated comic *KIM & KIM* from Black Mask Studio. She's also worked with Capstone, dedicated to juvenile literature, illustrating the books *Romeo and Juliet*, *Robinson Crusoe* and *The Three Musketeers*. She's done covers for the *Adventure Time* and *Bravest Warriors* licensed comic book series, and *Lumberjanes* for BOOM Studios! She founded the Boudika Comics studio along with Claudia Aguirre, where she published her own graphic novels, presenting them at national and international events such as Comic-Con in San Diego, Alternative Press Expo in San Francisco, and Guadalajara International Book Fair, among others. She is a vegan and lover of video games and animals.

behance.net/evacabrera / @evacabrera

CLAUDIA AGUIRRE is a queer comic book artist and writer. She is a GLAAD Award and Will Eisner Award nominee. She is also the co-founder of Boudika Comics, where she self-publishes comics. Currently, she is working for Black Mask, Oni Press, Legendary, Limerence Press, and Boom! Studios.

cargocollective.com/claudiaguirre / @claudiaguirre

CHRISTOPHER CRANK letters a bunch of books put out by Image, Dark Horse, Oni Press, and Dynamite. He also has a podcast with comic artist Mike Norton and members of Four Star Studios in Chicago (crankcast.net) and makes music (sonomorti.bandcamp.com).

@ccrank

MORE LIMERENCE PRESS TITLES...

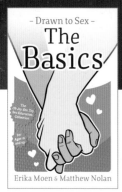
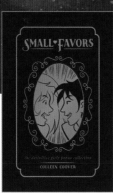
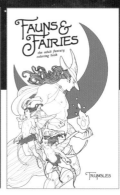
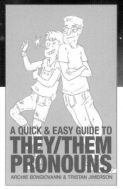

DRAWN TO SEX: THE BASICS
By Erika Moen and Matthew Nolan
ISBN 978-1-62010-544-3

SMALL FAVORS: THE DEFINITIVE GIRLY PORNO COLLECTION
By Colleen Coover
ISBN 978-1-62010-398-2

FAUNS & FAIRIES: THE ADULT FANTASY COLORING BOOK
By Trungles
ISBN 978-1-62010-403-3

A QUICK & EASY GUIDE TO THEY/THEM PRONOUNS
By Archie Bongiovanni & Tristan Jimerson
ISBN 978-1-62010-499-6

For more information on these and other fine Limerence Press comic books and graphic novels, visit www.onipress.com. To find a comic specialty store in your area, visit www.comicshops.us.